A TREK TO SOLOMON'S THRONE

1st Edition

Published in 2013 by
Woodfield Publishing Ltd
Bognor Regis PO21 5EL England
www.woodfieldpublishing.co.uk

ISBN 1-84683-149-0

Printed and bound in England

Typesetting & page layout | Nicole Pastorius
Cover design | Klaus Berger

A Trek to Solomon's Throne

& the Valley of the Assassins

Diary of a 1974 expedition to the Takht-e-Sulaiman Massif, Iran in the footsteps of Freya Stark

BRUCE BLACKNEY

Woodfield

Woodfield Publishing Ltd

Bognor Regis ~ West Sussex ~ England ~ PO21 5EL
tel 01243 821234 ~ **e/m** info@woodfieldpublishing.co.uk

Interesting and informative books on a variety of subjects

For full details of all our published titles, visit our website at
www.woodfieldpublishing.co.uk

This book is dedicated to the leaders of
British military adventurous training expeditions

All author's royalties from the sale of this book
will be donated to The Royal Air Force Benevolent Fund

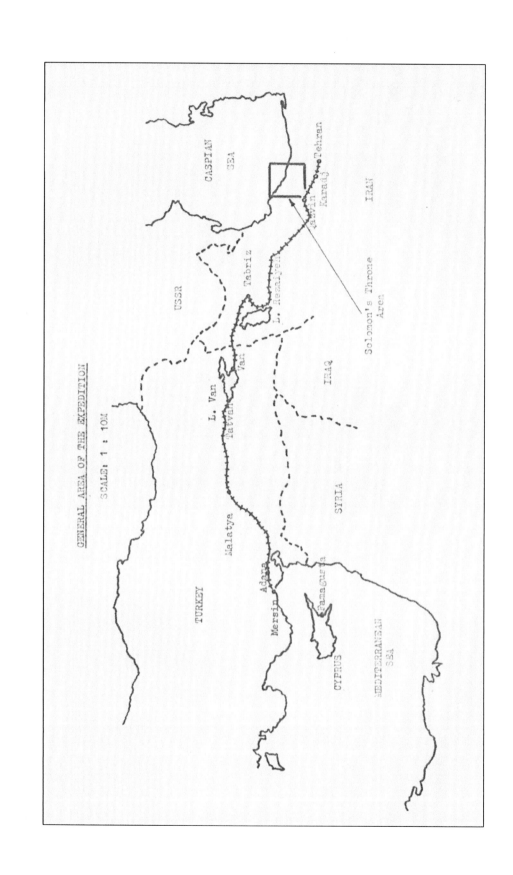

GENERAL AREA OF THE EXPEDITION

SCALE: 1 : 10M

~ CONTENTS ~

List of Illustrations

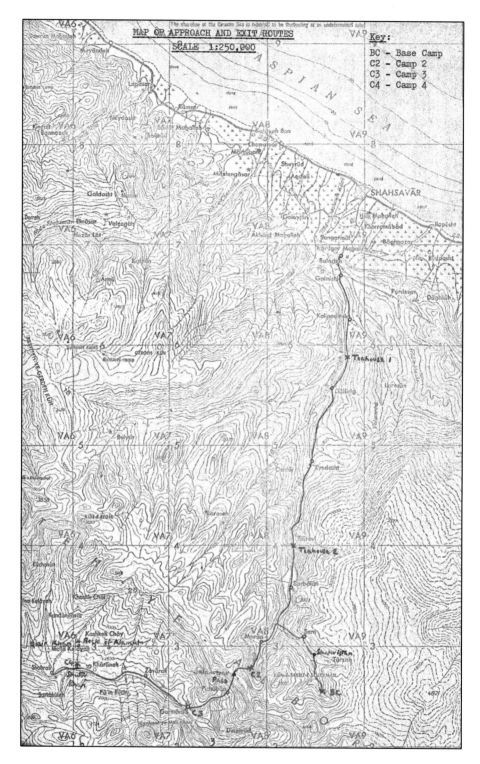

Map of approach and exit routes.

Foreword
by Sir Ranulph Fiennes, Bt, OBE

I first met Bruce Blackney in 1991 when he was General Manager for Airwork limited in the Sultanate of Oman. His enthusiasm for expeditions had not diminished and he readily helped my expedition to search for the lost city of Ubar by providing several volunteers from his organization with local knowledge of the deserts, caves and wildlife of Oman. In his spare time he drove an expedition Land Rover Discovery vehicle in the sand dunes of the Empty Quarter and participated in the archaeological digs for Ubar.

Solomon's Throne 1974 is a splendid example of an expedition organised by a small group of enthusiasts, in this case from RAF Akrotiri in Cyprus. It provided plenty of excitement and adventure for those taking part but could not have happened without meticulous planning. This book lays down the steps necessary in the planning of any expedition and emphasizes the importance of good reconnaissance and of a sustained training programme. The team showed that it jelled together and was able to cope with any emergency that arose. The objectives had been chosen well and the opportunity to follow in the footsteps of the explorer, Dame Freya Stark, was an added bonus. But it is fair to say that the success of the expedition would not have been so great without the excellent assistance from the Iran Special Forces. The ability to converse with muleteers and villagers en route was essential.

I believe that expeditions similar to Solomon's Throne 1974 are well within the scope of mountaineering, caving and trekking enthusiasts worldwide, particularly when they are organized within a structured organization such as the Armed Forces which support adventurous training activities. I recommend this book to all potential expedition leaders and to those who love adventure travel in the more remote areas of the World.

Ranulph Fiennes
2012

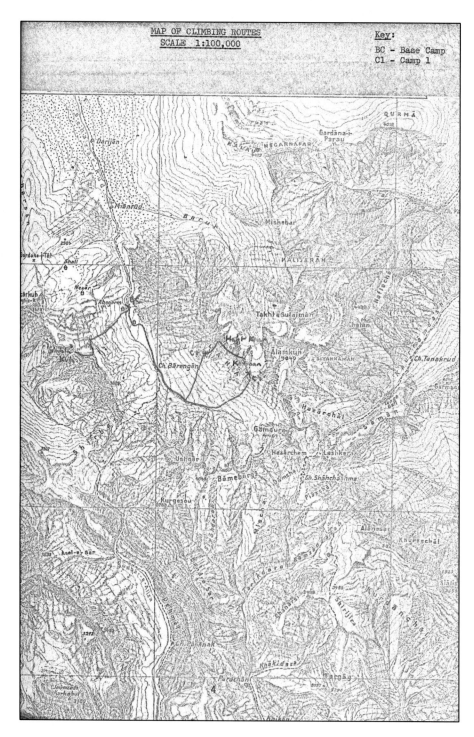

Map of climbing routes.

The Author

Bruce Blackney learnt his engineering skills as a student apprentice at the Royal Arsenal, Woolwich. After qualifying as a mechanical engineer he joined the P&O Line as an engineer officer and sailed on the Australia and Far East routes. This started his interest in foreign travel and adventure.

After marriage he joined the RAF in 1961 as an engineer officer and was the squadron engineer of Hunter fighter/ground attack squadrons. He served in Aden during the Radfan and South Arabian campaigns. He completed a postgraduate course at Cambridge and was seconded to the Ministry of Technology to undertake a technology survey in the USA. He

was involved in RAF expeditions to glaciers and ice caps in Norway.

In 1972 he was posted to RAF Akrotiri in Cyprus and was the Wing engineer for two Vulcan squadrons. Whilst there he continued his interest in expeditions and led an RAF team to climb the Solomon's Throne massif in Iran.

He later became the Chief Engineer at RAF Brize Norton and was promoted Group Captain to command an RAF Establishment in Norfolk and, subsequently, became an Assistant Director of the MoD. He retired from the RAF after 25 years and worked in the Sultanate of Oman as General Manager of Airwork Ltd – a large British company which provided engineering services to the Sultan's Armed Forces.

Whilst in Oman he helped Sir Ranulph Fiennes with his Ubar Expedition in the Empty Quarter. He has travelled extensively and has climbed and trekked in Morocco, South Africa, Malawi, Borneo and Lapland and in the Himalayas of India and Nepal. He took part in the RAF Mountaineering Association 50th Anniversary trek to Everest Base Camp in 1998.

Bruce now lives in a Sussex village and enjoys walking in the Weald and the South Downs.

Introduction

In 2011 the British Ambassador was expelled from Iran and violent crowds stormed and ransacked the British Embassy in Tehran. The Embassy was closed, as was the Iranian Embassy in London. The UK is seen as "Little Satan" by the ruling regime in Iran and British citizens are not welcome there.

But this has not always been the case... This book tells a story of Royal Air Force involvement in Iran in the early 1970s and how a British military expedition from RAF Akrotiri in Cyprus climbed the little known Iranian massif of 'Solomon's Throne' and also followed the footsteps of the famous British explorer, Freya Stark, in the Valley of the Assassins.

It reveals the splendid co-operation that existed between the Iranians and British at that time and also the hospitality and kindness demonstrated by ordinary Iranian citizens to the British visitors.

Bruce Blackney, 2013

1.   An Adventure Is Born

Iran Detachment

A thunderous roar deafened ears at Mehrabad Airport in Tehran, Iran. Four Vulcan bombers of No. 35 Squadron, Royal Air Force, rolled down the runway and took off one behind the other – their powerful Rolls Royce Olympus engines thrusting them into the sky. It was a splendid sight as the large delta winged aircraft flew overhead and disappeared into the distance.

It was 1972 and before the time of the Iranian Revolution. Iran was still ruled by Mohammed Reza Shah Pahlavi. It was a very different Iran from today and the country was mainly dependent on Western hardware, support and training for its armed forces.

No. 35 Squadron was based at RAF Akrotiri in Cyprus and was part of the shield of CENTO (Central Treaty Organization) forces attempting to contain the Cold War threat from the Soviet Union southern flank. CENTO was an organization similar to NATO and at that time the member states were the USA, the UK, Iran, Turkey and Pakistan.

A detachment from the squadron had been sent to Iran to exercise jointly with the Iranian Air Force. The detachment boss was the commanding officer of No. 35 Squadron, Wing Commander John Fitzpatrick. I was a squadron leader and the engineer officer of the detachment. I had a team of engineering, logistics and administration personnel and we operated from a tented camp on the airfield. Our job was to provide the support to allow the Vulcans to fly on their missions.

Fortunately we did not have to sleep in the hot and dusty conditions of the airfield. In fact it was highly dangerous to remain on the airfield after sunset. It was guarded by conscripted Iranian recruits whose orders were to shoot anything that moved. So we made quite sure that we were not there after dark.

After an exhausting day working in the heat we returned to our hotel in central Tehran. The detachment staff stayed in a hotel called the Elizabeth which was pleasant with comfortable facilities. Each morning we travelled to the airport in our khaki tropical uniforms and passed a group of pretty young Iranian chambermaids arriving for work at the hotel entrance. We could not help noticing that they giggled and flashed their eyelashes as they passed so many uniformed young men. Although the ladies clearly wanted to know us we resisted the temptation. We had been well briefed on Islamic customs and local laws. We knew that such fraternisation in a Muslim country was not allowed and would lead to problems.

The Muslim weekend was a time to relax and rest from our military duties. I suggested to another squadron leader and one of the squadron pilots that he may like to join me on a bus journey to the Caspian Sea which is some 100 miles to the north of Tehran. He had a lengthy classical Greek first name but I nicknamed him Phil. He readily agreed to join me so we cleared the trip with the boss.

On the Friday morning we set off very early and took a taxi to Tehran bus station. There we found a bus bound for Rasht via Amol and the Caspian coast. We purchased tickets for Rasht which would allow us to travel along the Caspian coast from East to West. Between Tehran and the Caspian were the Elburz Mountains – a range of spectacular mountains with snow covered peaks.

The drive through the mountains was incredibly beautiful and quite hair-raising with overhanging rocks and tunnels through the hillsides. At times the road seemed to teeter on the brink of a precipice and at others it wound precariously around bends so there was no chance of seeing traffic coming in the opposite direction. The most spectacular sight was Mount Damavand which at 18,638 feet was a peak of Himalayan proportions. Its snow covered summit was far above our line of sight and caused us to crane our necks looking upwards.

After we had been travelling through the mountains for a while the road began to descend to the small town of Amol. The bus stopped there and we descended to drink a glass of Iranian sweet tea (chai) at a roadside café. By this time we had got into conversation with an Iranian, Hossein, who was a passenger on the bus. He spoke a little English and was returning home after visiting Tehran. Hossein explained he had a house close to the Caspian Sea. He was most hospitable and insisted we visited his home. We explained we had tickets to Rasht but he said we could use the same ones on a later bus. So with some reluctance we agreed.

The scenery changed rapidly to green and lush vegetation as we descended to the Caspian coast. It was totally unlike the mountain scenery of the Elburz. Eventually Hossein indicated we should get off with him. We walked down a track to his house which was a single storey village house located in fields close to the sea. The climate was hot and humid and a complete contrast to the dry desert climate of Tehran. Soon we were introduced to Hossein's large family – including his wife, his parents, his grandparents, his sisters and the children.

Hossein explained that the ladies would prepare a meal and he suggested we walked down to the beach to see the Caspian Sea. There was a lovely sandy beach but it was completely deserted. The sun was shining and it was hot. The sea was calm and very blue. There was a surprising lack of boats. Hossein said that sometimes there were storms and the sea could be very rough.

We returned to Hossein's house where his mother and sisters had spread a large cloth on the floor. On it were dishes of yellow rice and others containing cooked meat. It was a type of chelo-kebab. We sat cross-legged on the wooden floor on Iranian carpets and ate with our right hands. There was a babble of Farsi in the room. The meal was superb and we sipped hot sweet tea (chai) as we chatted to those who understood a little English. The humidity was high and we sweated profusely. We ate slices of water melon to appease our thirst and spent our time swatting flies that were trying to eat us and our food!

The meal was a tremendous act of hospitality and we thanked Hossein profusely for his kindness. His family seemed genuinely honoured to be entertaining foreigners.

Phil and I caught another bus and travelled westwards towards Rasht. It was a long journey of more than 150 miles and it took us 3 to 4 hours of travelling along the Caspian coast. I kept glancing southwards towards the spectacular mountain backdrop of the Elburz Range. I was a mountaineer myself and had led RAF climbing expeditions in remote locations. I wondered whether these mountains could be the location of another great adventure for an RAF team. I was determined to investigate further when the time was right.

Eventually we reached the interesting ancient city of Rasht and discovered that there was a bus leaving later for Tehran. The bus followed the south easterly direct route to Tehran. Even so it was a long ride of more than 200 miles and it was 2am before we reached our hotel. Both Phil and I had enjoyed our adventure and felt we had learnt a little about our host country of Iran.

Cyprus Interlude

The Squadron detachment returned to Cyprus and resumed normal Cold War duties there. I was pre-occupied with engineering problems and organisational matters. However, when I had time, I reflected on all I had seen in Iran and the majesty of the Elburz Range. I knew that my climbing friend, Ray Condon, was being posted to Akrotiri very soon. Ray was a tall and angular Flight Lieutenant of the RAF Administration Branch. He and I had organised climbing and hill walking ventures when we were both based at the RAF Staff College at Bracknell in Berkshire. We had trained groups of RAF personnel in mountain climbing and trekking in the Welsh Mountains and the English Lake District.

I decided to suggest to Ray that we form an expedition club at RAF Akrotiri. "Expedition Training" as it was called was strongly supported by the military because it developed qualities of leadership, perseverance and self-reliance that were required in war situations. Provided it did not interfere with vital operational duties military personnel were allowed to participate in expeditions and were provided with essential rations and other support.

When Ray arrived in Cyprus we discussed the idea and he rapidly agreed. What we now needed was to recruit personnel who were interested in mountain activities. We organised a training programme and encouraged officers, airmen and airwomen to join us. We trained in the Troodos Mountains and at other locations in Cyprus where there were rock outcrops. Most weekends we were to be found rock climbing or trekking by compass through the pine forests of the Troodos. We also practised snow and ice techniques in winter and camped on the snow covered slopes of Mount Olympus.

Ray and I worked hard to build up our team. There was a good response from personnel of the RAF stations in Cyprus. We decided that our expedition prime objective would be to visit and climb the Solomon's Throne Massif in the Elburz range of Iran. So we set out a training programme for our Expedition Club members. We needed serious high mountain experience so we planned two short term expeditions – one to the Taurus Mountains of Southern Turkey and the other to climb Mount Idha in Crete.

Shiraz Inquiry

A short while before our team was due to leave for the Taurus Mountains I was appointed to be the engineer member of an RAF Board of Inquiry. An aircraft of another Vulcan squadron, No. 9, had crash landed and run off the runway at an Iranian Air Force base at Shiraz in Southern Iran. The Inquiry was headed by Wing Commander Alun Morgan and our job was to investigate the cause of the accident. Fortunately none of the Vulcan's crew had been killed or seriously injured.

Of course military duties took precedence over expeditions and I had to cancel my participation in the Taurus expedition and asked Ray to take over the leadership.

The Inquiry proceeded well and the Board established the technical failure that led to the crash. My team of technicians had to dig under the wreck of the aircraft to obtain evidence. Some parts disappeared over night and we suspected the Shiraz souk was doing a good trade in scrap metal. After that we insisted that the Iranian Air Force placed an armed guard on the wreck.

There was one amusing incident when we learnt that the Vulcan's navigator, who had mild concussion, had woken up in the local hospital to find that his nurse had fallen in love and wanted to marry him!

After all our investigations were complete and all witnesses interviewed the Board retired to our hotel in downtown Shiraz to write up our findings. We were invited to a social evening in the officers' mess of the Air Force base. I was amazed to find that it was almost identical to similar functions in an RAF officers' mess. There was good food and the latest western music and dancing – we thoroughly enjoyed ourselves.

When we had completely finished our work we had a spare day whilst we waited for a civil airways flight to Tehran. So we visited the ancient site of Persepolis and went to the evening son-et-lumière show there. Persepolis is about 40 miles from Shiraz and is located in the Zagros Mountains. The site is amazing because so much of it is still standing even though this ancient Persian city had been sacked by Alexander-the-Great and his advancing armies in 330 BC.

We watched the sun set over the Zagros Range. It was arid scenery but had its own beauty. Again I felt a longing to return to this fascinating country and to explore its mountains. I had a strange sense of déjà-vu and knew that in some way my destiny was linked to Iran and its mountains.

The son-et-lumière performance was really dramatic and quite eerie. This told the story of Persia's ancient empires and the kings (or shahs) who had ruled them. Some were buried in caves in the high mountains surrounding the site. As the commentator mentioned names such as Xerxes, Cyrus-the-Great and Darius-the Great their burial sites in the mountains were illuminated.

Abortive Trip

When I arrived back to our Cyprus base Ray and his team were still in Turkey and had a few days remaining there. I had arranged time off for the expedition so I thought I would join them and flew to Adana in Southern Turkey. After an overnight stay in an Adana hotel I took a local bus to a small town called Gülek and then boarded a mini bus travelling to the area at the base of the Taurus Range where I knew the expedition base camp should be set up. I had previously obtained diplomatic clearance for an RAF climbing and trekking expedition there from the Turkish authorities in Ankara.

I arrived at a small settlement near the base camp and enquired about my colleagues. At this stage a local gendarme appeared who spoke very limited English. I tried to explain about our climbing expedition and that the authorities in Ankara had approved it. The gendarme looked at me suspiciously and decided to arrest me. I had to accompany him to the village police station where he tried to question me on the reason I was there. He did not listen to my pleas about having permission from Ankara. He made a few phone calls in rapid Turkish – probably to his superiors. At this stage I was beginning to fear incarceration in a Turkish jail which I had heard could be pretty bad.

Eventually the gendarme made up his mind. I was forcibly made to sit in the rear of an open police vehicle and to sit next to an armed guard clutching a semi-automatic rifle. I was not in a position to argue but fortunately I retrieved my rucksack and gear. As no one in the vehicle spoke English I had no idea where I was being taken. However, my fears were unfounded as I was taken back to Gülek where I was released. It was simply a case of having been "run out of town" – clearly I was not welcome!

By then it was getting dark and I had to find somewhere to stay. There was only one decrepit building labelled "Ötel" in the whole town. It was distinctly "sleazy" but I had no choice. After ringing a hand bell at reception I was shown a room and told it was the last available. When I saw it I cringed at the state of the bed and the furnishings. I am sure every type of bug lived in the dirty sheets. I ended up lying on the cold stone floor in my sleeping bag and listening to the rats scurrying around me. I didn't sleep a wink that night!

After such an experience I escaped back to Adana and nearby Mersin – the port for Cyprus. I took the first ferry to Famagusta and returned to base.

Ray and his team eventually returned. They had had a similar experience with local officialdom and had been diverted to a totally different area of the Taurus Range. However, they had managed to get in some good climbing and trekking.

Crete

The second part of our mountaineering training was to climb Mount Idha in Crete in snow conditions. This time I managed to get away without interruption from service duties. Our small team of eight expeditioners flew to Athens over the Greek Easter period. All were members of the Akrotiri Expedition Club and, apart from Ray and I, comprised Mike Dawson, Phil Sperring, John Harrison, Clive (Locky)) O'Loughlin, Roger Kelsey and Eddy Kemp.

We called on the British Defence Attaché and advised him of our plans. We then went to the port of Piraeus and took the night boat to Crete. As we approached the island we had a clear view of our objective – the snow covered peak of Mount Idha which dominated the skyline behind the port of Heraklion. It looked daunting when viewed from the sea.

We had already been in contact with the Cretan Mountaineering Club and we called one of its principal members. It was rather like a scene from a John le Carré novel. He insisted we meet him in a dry cleaners' shop in the narrow back streets of the city. We tracked him down and discovered the reason for the strange venue – he was the owner of the shop! He was very welcoming and wished us well on our climb.

We then took a bus to the small village of Kamares, near Platanos, which was to the south of Mount Idha. We found a large room to sleep in and we managed to locate some mules which we could use for the first part of our trek through the foot hills of the mountain. These were not essential but would give us good experience of using mules in Iran.

We spent the evening drinking Greek coffee in the village coffee shop. Many of the locals appeared to be in an alcoholic haze for Greek Easter. They had red crosses marked on their foreheads. But the most amazing meeting was with a group of elderly and wizened Cretan men. They could speak a little English and told us they were partisans during World War II. They related the story of when they captured the German commandant of the Island during the occupation. The partisans spirited the commandant through the mountains and on to a British submarine. He was later imprisoned at Beaconsfield in England.

Of course the reprisals for this audacity were horrific – all the inhabitants of one Cretan village were executed! As we listened to the story we felt rather glad we were not a group of German climbers.

The following morning we made our attempt on Mount Idha (8065 ft). The first part was straightforward and the terrain was rocky. Eventually the route became too difficult for mules and we unloaded them and carried our rucksacks, food and camping gear. We bade farewell to the muleteers and continued climbing upwards. The route was a steep scramble through boulder fields until we reached the snow line. After this we donned crampons and carried ice axes. It was slow going but not difficult. The main problem was the weather which was deteriorating badly with a blizzard developing. We were approaching the summit which we could just discern ahead through the blanket of snow. But then we hit "white out" conditions. I called a halt and insisted we set up camp. It would be impossible to reach the summit until the visibility cleared.

We pitched our four lightweight tents having cut out platforms in the snow. We made a brew and cooked an evening meal. We were now warm and snug in our sleeping bags. However, an electric storm was developing which was one of the worst I have ever experienced in the mountains. The lighting was flashing around the boulders surrounding our camp with claps of thunder every few minutes. There was a strong electric field and our hair stood on end. I was concerned that our tents would be struck. I insisted that those in the tents with light alloy poles transferred to the tents with plastic poles. So there were four of us lying on each other in two man tents. It was scarcely the most peaceful night in our lives!

Eventually the storm subsided and at daybreak we peered outside. Although we were buried in deep snow and had to dig ourselves out the visibility was clear in the early morning sunshine. We discovered we were just below the summit of Mavri – one of the peaks of Mount Idha. The storm had damaged one of our tents and had broken a ridge pole.

Ray had got up early and was making tea for everyone. He had gone around collecting all the water bottles. To his surprise there were voluble reactions to the brew. Only then did he remember that one of the water bottles had contained some 'medicinal' vodka to keep out the cold on the mountain! It certainly woke people up quickly.

The View from Mavri at dawn

When we were up and had eaten breakfast the sky was clear and calm but we saw clouds rising up from the valleys below and soon realized that the weather was about to change again. We broke camp quickly and roped up ready for the descent – it was too dangerous to attempt the short route to the summit. Soon after we were in total 'white out' and could only see a few feet ahead. Fortunately Mike and Ray had made a mental note of the compass bearing we would need to make a safe descent. The long, cold descent took its toll. John, who was of slight build, was suffering from the onset of hypothermia, and both Mike and Ray, who were taking the lead in the teams, received frost nip to fingers and toes.

We were descending on a different route to our climb but when we arrived at Kamares the locals were amazed that we had survived as it was the worst storm on the mountain in living memory. They had considered calling out the Mountain Rescue team to save us but they were not willing to go anywhere near the mountain.

At the village we drank a celebratory glass of retzina and chatted to the villagers. We spent the rest of the day climbing some spectacular rock outcrops nearby. The following day we went to see a spectacular gorge called the Vorizia Farangi and climbed down through it. On our last day we visited the ancient Cretan city of Knossos near Heraklion and were very impressed by its buildings and the cult of bull jumping.

We went on to Heraklion where we were invited to dinner in the club room of the Cretan Mountaineering Club. This was really amusing. After the dinner Cretans kept toasting us in Ouzu. They emptied their glasses rapidly and placed the upturned glasses on their heads. We followed suit but with more discretion – I had warned the guys what to expect. As the night wore on some of the Cretans started slipping under the table completely "out of their minds". We all "crashed out" on the club room floor! It was with seriously bad hangovers that our team boarded the ferry back to Piraeus!

Reconnaissance

Ray and I continued our planning for an expedition to Iran and we researched all possible information about the Elburz Range. Unfortunately in those days there was no Internet and no search engines such as Google to help us. We had to rely on books from libraries and other sources. We also obtained comprehensive maps of the Elburz from military sources.

What we did find out was that the famous English woman explorer, Freya Stark, had visited the Elburz Range in the 1930s and was the first English woman to do so. We obtained a copy of her book "The Valleys of the Assassins." She had visited the Alamut Valley which was close to the Solomon's Throne massif and she had lived with the locals in their villages. We learned that for nearly 150 years during the Middle Ages the secret society of the Assassins had operated from the Alamut Valley and used subterfuge, intimidation, and even assassination to control the Middle East from Syria to Persia. The Assassins were well known for taking Hashish (hence assassin) and famous for their murderous role in eliminating enemies. This appeared to be the origin of the name "assassin".

We decided that one of the secondary objectives of the expedition should be to visit the Valley of the Assassins and to see if any of the local tribes' people remembered Freya Stark's visit. We would aim to visit the Assassins' former stronghold at the Rock of Alamut.

Freya Stark also told us what Persian folklore said about Solomon's Throne. "King Solomon married the Queen of Sheba but he was old and she was young and he couldn't get her to love him. So he commanded the birds to go out and find the coldest place on earth. All but the Hoopoe returned next morning but the Hoopoe did not return until evening. The Hoopoe apologised and said his wings had been frozen to the ground on a mountain top and he could not fly until the sun warmed them. So the King set up his tent at that place and the Queen was so cold she had to share the King's tent. The next morning the King struck the ground and a hot spring gushed up where the Queen could bathe. The mountain is called Solomon's Throne in the Elburz to the South of the Caspian and the hot spring is called Ab-e-Garm".

We had many unanswered questions. It soon became clear that we would need to have a reconnaissance to Iran to obtain answers – not the least being whether the British and Iranian governments would allow us to mount the expedition.

I had some leave due and planned a short trip to Tehran via an RAF VC10. For this I could apply for an indulgence flight on a "spare seat" basis. There was no suitable VC10 return flight from Tehran but I managed to obtain a seat on an RAF Hercules which was leaving from Mashad near the Afghanistan border a few days later. I hoped I would be able to take a bus from Tehran to Mashad even though it was a long journey.

I asked for a meeting with the Defence Attaché and the Assistant Military Attaché at the British Embassy. I sent them signals (military telex) to explain our proposals to hold the expedition and to request that permission be sought from the Iranian Government and military. I told them my travel arrangements but this met with a rebuttal – apparently the Iranian authorities did not allow passengers to join RAF flights at Mashad. However, an alternative was suggested that I should travel by train from Tehran to Kayseri in central Turkey from where I could reach Mersin and the ferry to Cyprus.

I rapidly agreed the revised travel plan and Major Arthur Gooch, the Assistant Military Attaché, promised to obtain a ticket for a couchette from Tehran to Kayseri if I refunded him in due course.

The VC10 flight to Tehran was uneventful and Arthur met me at the airport and took me to the Embassy. I discussed the expedition with him at length. He said he could arrange transport on repayment and a campsite for our nights in Tehran. He also agreed to receive and store the British composite (compo) military rations which would be our food supplies for the expedition. These were the equivalent of the US military rations (MREs &c). Most importantly Arthur had a store where the expedition team could change into trekking gear and leave our casual travelling gear whilst we were "on the hill". Arthur gave me the rail tickets to Kayseri and I duly paid him.

I also went in to see Arthur's boss, Group Captain Primavesi, who was the Defence Attaché and two ranks senior to me. At first the atmosphere was frosty and I got a "rollicking" for assuming I could join the Hercules at Mashad. However, as I explained our expedition plans to the Group Captain he warmed to the ideas and gave them his full support. He did say that if the Iranians gave permission they may wish to send some of their own military personnel to join the expedition. This idea left me feeling a little unsure but it was really a case of "wait and see" how they performed and jelled with our team. Certainly to have Farsi speakers with us would be extremely valuable.

I stayed at the Elizabeth Hotel again and on the second day I took an early bus to the Caspian coast. My mission was to establish whether it was possible to hire mules and muleteers for the expedition's journeys through the Elburz. We had tents, compo rations and mountaineering gear to move, which amounted to a considerable weight.

Ray and I had already planned the location of the base camp and the trekking routes we would follow. We were unsure of the accuracy of the maps and whether the routes were in existence. However, it seemed feasible to start the "walk-in" to base camp from near the small town of Khorramabad on the Caspian coast.

I got off the bus at Khorramabad where I saw a track disappearing south towards the Elburz. I could see some mules and muleteers at the start of the track. So clutching a Farsi dictionary I went across to speak to them in a mixture of Farsi and English. After great difficulty I established that they took mule trains to the Takht-e-Sulaiman region of the Elburz. What I could not do was establish the prices they charged – evidently this was for negotiation and I could now see the sense of having the Iranian military with us. At least I felt confident that this was the right start point for the expedition's "walk-in".

I returned to Tehran and prepared to catch the morning train to Turkey. The Imperial Iranian Railways had a reputation for prompt departures. Accordingly I arrived early for the train at Tehran's central station. I checked in and received my ticket for Kayseri. I found myself allocated to a couchette that slept four. My companions were an elderly German and his wife and a voluble Frenchman. I spoke some French but no German whereas the Frenchman spoke some German. The Germans spoke no English or French. So we communicated in strange relayed messages which were often translated twice.

I managed to get a top bunk since the Germans were elderly and could not climb up to it. There was a dining car on the train so I went for some breakfast. When I returned I spoke to my companions and established that the Germans were tourists and the Frenchman was on business. They had one thing in common – they both needed to make an aircraft connection in Ankara.

We journeyed throughout the day and I was interested to see the scenery of North Western Iran and views of the old city of Tabriz. I listened to the voices and accents at stations we stopped at and realised that people were no longer speaking Farsi but a version of Azeri – a Turkic language. It was nightfall when we approached the Turkish border but here the train was shunted into a siding and remained there all night. I could tell that my travelling companions were becoming annoyed at the delay. There was no explanation from the train staff of what was happening. I was not concerned since I had four days before I needed to report for duty at RAF Akrotiri.

At daybreak we were visited by train officials to examine our tickets. They said that the delay was because we were waiting to pass a train in the opposite direction on a single line. The train coming from Turkey was seriously delayed. We spent the second morning moving a short way and then waiting in another siding.

I managed a long conversation with my companions in the couchette. The German man was apparently a former "storm trooper" in Hitler's army during World War II. The Frenchman was a businessman in Paris. They both displayed national characteristics about the delay. The German swore in German at any train officials who passed by along the corridor and the

Frenchman lent out of the window and hurled abuse in rapid French at any railway employee in sight. The situation became extremely heated. Fortunately I could remain calm and observe the antics of my companions. I became bored with their impatience and went to the dining car for coffee.

Eventually, when the train was nearly a day late, it arrived at the Turkish border and immigration officials examined our passports. Fortunately I was able to surrender the infamous pink form issued on arrival in Iran. Without this a foreigner could not leave the country. We moved slowly over the border and stopped again for the Turkish officials to examine and stamp passports.

In Eastern Turkey the scenery was spectacular with dramatic mountain views and large rivers. The people looked distinctly Turkish with men wearing flat caps and shoes with curled up toes. The fields had carts hauled by bullocks with solid wooden wheels – rather like the carts of the Roman Empire. Villages with groups of black tents were visible from the train. I assumed that these were peopled by Kurdish tribes' people.

At Lake Van we transferred to a ferry and joined another train after the voyage. The lake was vast and like an inland sea. I enjoyed stretching my legs and walking around the ship. Turkish music was playing and I ate snacks of Turkish food which were excellent.

The train continued slowly through Turkey and was a day late by the time it reached Malatya. At each major station it waited a long time so I walked along the platform to a ticket office. I discovered there was a "postal" train which connected with the train from Tehran and went direct to Adana and near to Mersin, the port for Cyprus. However, I had time to spare so I continued my journey to Kayseri.

I finally left the train at Kayseri station and bade the Frenchman and the German couple farewell. They were still cursing about the loss of a whole day. I sympathized and wished them well.

I went to the bus station and found that there were buses to Adana and Mersin via Göreme. I knew that Göreme was the centre for Cappadocia. I had a day to spare so I stayed there and explored the fascinating karst country of hundreds of small sharp pointed limestone peaks. Many were riddled with caves which had been inhabited by early Christians. Some had Christian paintings on the cave walls and I visited one which had been a church.

I arrived in Mersin and took the ferry to Famagusta. I rode in a "share-taxi" and soon arrived back at Akrotiri. I telephoned Ray to brief him on the outcome of my reconnaissance.

Final Preparations

For almost eighteen months Ray and I had worked to recruit Expedition Club members and, where necessary, to train them to become proficient in the arts of the mountaineer – rock climbing, fell-walking, compass navigation and survival.

At last, a group of hardy mountain types emerged from the rigours of the training programme to provide a nucleus for the long awaited expedition. The selection of the final list of members was not an easy task – not only did they have to be competent mountaineers and capable of blending into a team, but their commanding officers had to be persuaded to release them from normal duty for the period of the expedition. However, by April 1974 twelve volunteers were assembled for briefing and preparation of kit.

All the members were from RAF stations in Cyprus, and it included two members of the fair sex – Cherry Dowdeswell and Edith Fisher; both of the Women's Royal Air Force (WRAF). Edi, a physical training instructress with a "Geordie" accent, was so fit that she put us all to shame. Cherryl, a dark-haired Welsh lass with a "Birmingham" accent, competed on equal terms with the men on any rock face.

Of the men, Vic Last was a professional physical education officer who was powerfully built and with all the staying power required of a mountain man. Our doctor, John Dove, was a man with a great sense of humour. He was relatively new to the Service and still had the manner of a junior house surgeon at a London hospital. Peter Fields, the expedition hygienist, was a great expert on all Middle Eastern health hazards. To the forefront of our climbing team was Mike Dawson – a very competent leader on severe routes and a member of the Near East Air Force Mountain Rescue Team (MRT). He was backed up by Locky O'Loughlin and Eddy Kemp, who were also members of the MRT. Our expedition group was completed by Roger Kelsey, a cook by trade, and Malcolm Simmonds, a newcomer to the climbing fraternity.

There was a flurry of activity in our club store at Akrotiri. All equipment for the major expedition needed to be checked and tested. There were a number of other matters yet to be resolved. The first was the question of expedition length. We knew that too long a timescale would result in the members being denied release from normal military duties. So we settled on an overall time of 18 days. The other question was travel to and from Iran. Although there was a good chance of getting seats on an RAF aircraft for the outbound journey this was unlikely to happen for the return journey – at least not to suit our overall timescale. So we decided to return overland by train from Tehran to Turkey since I had already proved the route during my reconnaissance. However, this time we would change to the "postal" train from Malatya to Mersin. We would ask Arthur Gooch at the British Embassy to reserve our tickets.

We received official notification from the Iranian authorities giving us permission to mount the expedition. We were also advised that we would be accompanied by a detachment from the Iranian Special Forces. We were delighted and honoured to be given assistance at such a level.

At the beginning of June 1974 all planning had been completed and our logistic problems resolved by the offer of seats on an RAF VC 10 aircraft flying to Tehran on 14 June. We sent a signal to Arthur Gooch to reserve seats on the train departing Tehran on 27 June. One thing remained to be done – a trial to be organised for a drug company who had asked us to test some of their products under expedition conditions.

At long last the departure day approached. In the flurry of final briefings and last minute packing, we had little time to feel apprehensive about the challenge ahead.

2. Journey to the Caspian

14 June 1974

Twelve figures laden by rucksacks and climbing paraphernalia stood pensively in the Air Movements Lounge at RAF Akrotiri contemplating the unknown adventures of the forthcoming weeks. Life-long friends would doubtless be made, disasters might occur and, who knew whether we would all come back to tell the tale. It was midday on 14 June, and Akrotiri's Solomon's Throne Expedition had at last assembled for the journey to Tehran. Was this to be an anti-climax after the months of planning and patient waiting? I must admit that I felt a few nagging doubts at the enormity of our objectives and whether they could be achieved. Such thoughts were soon jarred from doubting minds by a harsh booming from the public address loud speakers which called on all passengers for Flight 2329 to assemble in the Departure Lounge. So the game was finally on!

The Team: L to R: Mike, Eddy, Ray,
Locky, John, Roger, Pete, Bruce
Cherryl, Edi, Vic, Malcolm

Farewells said and photographers satisfied, the team climbed aboard the gleaming VC10 aircraft of RAF Strike Command and we were soon winging our way skywards to Tehran and the mysteries of the Persian hinterland. The flight was uneventful and it seemed no time at all before the dun coloured ridges of the Iranian steppe loomed up on the approach to Tehran's Mehrabad Airport.

After landing confusion reigned and, for a while, we began to wonder whether the next few weeks would be spent taxiing around the perimeter of the International Airport. But not so – it soon became evident that the pilot was searching for the strip of red carpet that led to the VIP pavilion! Somewhat surprised at such a reception, we gazed in awe at the assembled "brass hats" resplendent in their best Iranian uniforms. But alas, such fame was not for us and we soon learnt that our aircraft was carrying no less a person than the Vice Chief of the British Defence Staff.

The VC10 was soon to taxi again – this time to the Passenger Terminal – and before long we emerged in the bright sunlight of a Tehran June afternoon. In the crowd below, Major Arthur Gooch, the Assistant Military Attaché I had met during the reconnaissance, was waving furiously. A quick few words of greeting and then we were whisked away in an airport bus to complete the formalities of immigration and customs.

Passports were duly stamped and pink entry forms obtained, for without these it was impossible to leave Iran. At this stage we were somewhat dismayed to find Mike Dawson and Peter Fields being led away by a fierce-looking airport policeman and to disappear into a small office. Fearing the worst, I moved forward to negotiate their release. But all was well – it was simply a case of their passport photographs not being true likenesses of their more haggard features of today

Customs posed no difficulties and, as we collected our baggage, we suddenly became aware of three smartly attired Iranian soldiers in mottled camouflage combat suits who were standing discreetly aside from the crowd in the terminal. Surely these were our liaison team? As Ray and I approached, a captain in a peaked "Foreign Legion" style cap and Ranger flashes on his sleeve stepped forward and introduced himself as Captain Yaghoob Aliary of the 1st Battalion Special Forces, Imperial Iranian Army. His team comprised Sergeant Major Ahmed Zamanpour and Sergeant Mohammed Ali-Regaie.

They looked tough and able mountain troops and we were to realise in the weeks to come that they were more than a match for our fitness – despite our weeks of training. The Iranian Special Forces are the equivalent of our Special Air Services (SAS) and Captain Ali, as we were to call him, proudly announced that he had completed the US Army's "Green Beret" training course in the USA. From that moment on we had no doubts about the service we were to receive, and Captain Ali emphasized this in a speech of welcome to all our party. We also learnt that his sergeant major was a climbing instructor to the Special Forces, and his sergeant was to be our radio operator. We had not been allowed to bring our own radio sets and it was reassuring to know that the Iranians were providing these.

At this stage we realised we had lost contact with Arthur Gooch whom we had expected to meet outside the Customs Hall. After a thorough search, we located a rather exhausted Arthur who had evidently been confronted with two major problems – the loss of the Vice Chief's baggage, and the need to find overnight accommodation in busy Tehran for an aircraft load of passengers after it had been discovered that an engine of our VC10 could not be re-started. At this news, the team gasped at their good fortune for the fate of the stranded passengers could equally have been theirs at Akrotiri.

We never did establish how Arthur resolved his problems. Nevertheless, he soon found the mini-bus he had hired for our travels in Iran and our kit was swiftly loaded aboard. Ray and I travelled in an ancient staff car which at some stage of its long life had been proudly driven by the Station Commander of the now-closed RAF Sharjah in the Gulf. The rest of the party followed in the mini-bus and soon we were to come to grips with the hair-brained drivers in Tehran's traffic. Iranian drivers describe their traffic dodging as equivalent to the competition of the football field and, before five minutes had elapsed, all of us could see why. Most of the team were somewhat surprised to reach the safety of the British Embassy gates unscathed.

The Embassy was the place for a rapid change into mountaineering kit and to collect our heavy equipment and rations which had been air freighted to Tehran some weeks earlier. We learnt with dismay that Iranian Customs had made a charge on one consignment but, fortunately, it was not too exorbitant. In the gathering darkness the team completed the loading of the mini-bus and the baggage on the roof rack assumed mountainous proportions. Eventually, all was roped on and we were soon on our way to the official camping site some six miles south west of Tehran at Gol-e-Sahra.

The expedition proper had begun and now was the time for the relaxed atmosphere that accompanies such a venture. I was known as "the major" to the Iranians where only Army ranks are understood. So, following the example of the well-known British Army expedition leader, Lt Col Blash-ford-Snell, I donned a gleaming white pith helmet. Some said it was reminiscent of Livingstone's last journey but I rather hoped not since he did not return! After the last of the ribald comments from Vic Last on his plans for Bruce's hat, there was a chance to survey the rest of the motley crew on the bus. Ray's tall figure was adorned with a Tryolean hat perched jauntily on his head, while in his hand he clutched a stout stick embossed by badges from Austrian Alpine huts. Roger Kelsey wore his famous "ding-a-ling" – a sheep scare that jangled bells at his every move. Most of the rest were gaily attired in a variety of bush hats but undoubtedly Malcolm Simmonds boasted the most brightly coloured version in a shade of "luminous orange." Our new-found Iranian colleagues were amused by the strange ways of the British and were obviously experiencing some difficulty sizing us up!

Gol-e-Sahra was reached at 9pm and we found it to be a small camp site frequented by caravaners, students and hippies. Examples of the "flower people's" graffiti were evident on some walls, but otherwise the site was well kept and the brick built ablutions were clean and of a reasonable standard. The team soon found a small grass enclosure hedged in by high bushes and bedded down for the night. Both temperature and humidity were high and there was no need for tents but, as a precaution against mosquito bites, most of us crawled inside our somewhat hot mountain sleeping bags.

The night was disturbed by the noise of locomotive sirens from the nearby railway track. Even more "earth shattering" was the arrival of a fierce-looking local cat which landed spitting and squawking in our midst. The camp was soon entertained by moonlight glimpses of Ray pursuing this monster with his stick in "great white hunter" style. Fortunately the RSPCA were not around to witness this obvious infringement of their code!

15 June 1974

The time was 4am and dawn not yet broken. A throbbing engine announced the arrival of our mini-bus and the team were soon up and about preparing a light breakfast and stacking equipment on the bulging roof-rack. By 5am we were speeding through the busy streets of the city and passed the imposing Shahyad Monument in its gleaming white ferro-concrete. The bus stopped at a traffic control before speeding along the Karadj Freeway westbound from Tehran. Meanwhile, inside the vehicle our conversation flowed from discussion of Tehran's reckless drivers to the unknown perils which faced us in the days to come. Captain Ali's English improved and we soon had him developing an appreciation for our brand of humour. Unfortunately, our jokes were lost on Sergeant Regaie, who spoke little English, and on Sergeant Major Zamanpour who spoke none at all.

After the small town of Karadj, the mini-bus turned north and immediately began climbing a steep-sided mountain valley. The rushing white waters of a river to our right brought thoughts of waterborne expeditions to the canoeists in our midst. The scenery soon became even grander and high mountains dominated the scene as we climbed to cross the majestic Elburz Range. Hairpin bends became the norm and before long the imposing retaining wall of the Karadj Dam loomed into view. Trapping millions of gallons of water in a steep-sided mountain valley, the dam is a playground for Tehran's nouveau riche. Gaily coloured house boats are strung along the sides and aquatic sports are obviously in vogue.

Captain Ali drew our attention to the use made of the dam by his Special Forces Group. High wires some 600 feet above the water level were stretched across the valley. We stopped the bus to study this phenomenon as it was explained that these were used for parachute training. The trainees are evidently launched on pulleys suspended from the high wire and, when they are at the lowest point of the catenary, they jump releasing their parachutes to brake their fall into the cold waters of the dam. Apparently all recruits to the Special Forces undertake this training. Only the parachutists in our team, Edi Fisher and Mike Dawson, expressed any regrets at not being able to try the jump for themselves.

Back again in the bus, we climbed higher still until snow-capped peaks of over 13,000 feet were added to the grandeur of the scene. Snow tunnels protected the road from the winter's onslaught and at one point, at a height of nearly 8,500 feet, the road plunged into a long tunnel illuminated by white neon strip lighting along its length. We were fascinated at the effectiveness of the insulation on these lights since the whole roof of the tunnel was running with water from underground mountain springs.

By now we had crossed the highest point of the pass and began the descent to the Caspian Sea Coast. The Caspian is below normal sea-level and the journey down to the coast would involve a much greater change in height than we had experienced on the climb from Tehran – a city at 4000 feet above sea level. The northern side of the range is completely different in character to the southern side. The heavy rainfall in this region has transformed the brown and grey rocks of the steppe into green grass-covered slopes and, at lower level, the terrain is covered by a dense temperate rain forest. The contrast is astounding, and for all the party except the Muslims, it was – to draw a Biblical parallel – like entering the Garden of Eden from the Wilderness.

Just below the top of the pass we stopped for chai – Iranian tea – at a small village. This was our first chance to sample the hot brown liquid that was to quench our thirst on many an occasion in the days ahead. The air in the village was cool and refreshing and a complete contrast from Tehran's dusty plains. Our time to explore was limited to finding out whether the dusty outhouse to the rear of the wayside café was there for the purpose we supposed! Fortunately our guess was correct and before long we were back in the bus and negotiating the hairpin bends of an incredibly steep descent. Magnificent rock slabs of several thousand feet were revealed and roused the climbing spirit in every member of the expedition. At one point we reached the top of a stupendous gorge in which the road could be viewed some 2,000 feet vertically below and four hairpin bends later. At another, cliffs of volcanic rock overhung the road in tortured folds and looked just like some primeval triumphant archway.

The landscape had changed to more gentle slopes thickly clad with lush green forest when we stopped in a forest park near Chalus to stretch our legs. This was a delightful glade reminiscent of English woodland with birdsong echoing through the trees. A broad river, the Rudkhaneh-e-Chalus, flowed by in the background. With memories of dry and dusty Cyprus bondu still fresh in our minds, this beautiful place seemed like a glimpse of paradise.

The next stop was Chalus at another traffic control. Evidently they have an effective system for monitoring traffic regulations in Iran. Captain Ali swiftly came to our driver's aid when an Iranian policeman complained that our mini-bus was overloaded. The captain explained that our team were visitors to Iran and should not be hindered. As if by magic, the policeman vanished and we had no more trouble. But our interest was revived by the knowledge that the border of the Soviet Union was across the Caspian Sea. Not surprisingly, no boats were to be seen on its surface, but the beaches were obviously a popular spot for holidaymakers. Gaily coloured villas surrounded by beautiful gardens were much in evidence.

At about 11am we approached the small coastal resort of Shahsavar and turned inland on a road to Khorramabad. The road passed through a landscape of lush green meadows as it crossed the coastal plain. Sheltered by groups of trees were square-shaped hay barns perched on stilts – obviously to raise the drying fodder above swamps which were liable to extensive flooding. The houses we saw were mainly of wood construction with steeply slanted corrugated iron or thatched roofs to drain off the very heavy rainfall in this region. After seeking directions at the small township of Khorramabad, the mini-bus headed further south down an earth track until we reached the small village of Baladeh, our destination. From here we were to hire mules for the trek to base camp.

3.   Through The Rain Forest

We came to a halt near a wooden house on the south side of the village. After unloading we instructed the mini-bus driver to meet us by midday on the 25 June at the village of Shahrak at the Western end of the Valley of the Assassins. Ray and I then set out with Captain Ali to negotiate with the muleteers we had noticed tending their animals in the main street. We learnt with dismay that no man was prepared to take us that day. The mule trains return to the village during the afternoon and their drivers were not anxious to reverse their steps. Despite numerous 'Salaams' and other salutations, the 'charvadars'- as the muleteers are known in Farsi – remained stubborn. Captain Ali believed the only way he could influence the situation was to obtain the assistance of the local gendarme.

This seemed a sensible idea, so Captain Ali, Ray and I set out to visit the gendarmerie post. According to Captain Ali, it was just up the steep track that led up a small hill south of the village. As events proved, this was the greatest under-exaggeration of all time! To recount the story:

Leaders' Recce of Baladeh

"We soon learnt that the captain moved like a human engine with pistons at full speed. The humidity was extremely high and, by the top of the rise, both Ray and I were sweating profusely and beginning to suffer from the first stages of heat exhaustion. We were evidently most unwise to try to compete with the Iranians who were far more used to these conditions.

The scenery changed dramatically on the south side of the hill. A large area of terraced rice paddy fields stretched before us and the verdant landscape reminded us both of Malaysia. Before we could reach the paddy fields we had to pass through a small copse and cross two fast flowing rivers – the second on a most precarious and rickety wood-pole bridge. Brightly coloured large dragon-flies were in profusion and the reds and blues of their bodies shimmered in the heat as they hovered over pools of stagnant water.

After walking up the bed of a muddy stream, our group of three emerged on a footpath which criss-crossed the rice paddy. Several village women clad in colourful red and yellow dresses worn over rolled-up long black cotton trousers stood knee-deep in the rice fields. Although they did not wear the chador – the Muslim veil – we noticed they averted their faces from our gaze despite our friendly 'Salaams.' This custom was to change the further we penetrated into the mountains and, in remote villages, the women laughed and joked openly before the British strangers.

The rice fields were to prove more interesting than we had supposed. In the course of 50 yards we had seen the heads of three snakes emerge from the water-logged paddy to watch us pass. Another, about 3 feet long, wriggled across the narrow path before us. Fortunately, we had been told by Captain Ali that this type was unlikely to be dangerous although those in the mountains were. After passing several houses on stilts and another hour later, we began to wonder whether we would ever reach the promised gendarmerie. But our fears were soon dispelled; we entered the first trees of the forest and emerged in a small hamlet of wooden houses with chickens clucking as they scattered out of the way; our 'short walk' had taken nearly one and a half hours!

The gendarmerie post was a small house surmounted by the Iranian flag at the far end of a group of wooden buildings. Captain Ali made some enquiries only to find that the resident gendarme had gone up-country to recover the body of a tribesman who had fallen in the river near Ab-e-Garm – the planned site of our base camp. The only occupant of the post was a teacher-soldier; a young educated national serviceman who had been sent to teach the villagers to read and write under the Iranian Government's literacy campaign.

Evidently he was instructed by Captain Ali to find mules for our team. However, he must have given the wrong answer for the next we knew he was standing stiffly to attention before the captain and receiving a severe dressing down. He looked most unhappy and we could not help but feel sorry for him. Secretly, we suspected that this was a show of force by the captain to demonstrate his power before the gathering crowd of villagers.

After this outburst, we sat down outside a small chaikhana – an Iranian village teahouse – to discuss the situation with the headman over a small glass of chai. After the fifth glass and feeling much refreshed from the steamy heat that had engulfed us on our journey, we began to make some progress. The villagers could possibly round up eight mules and send them with muleteers to our group at Baladeh. After another round of tea and much haggling over prices, we extracted a promise that they would send the mules and muleteers as soon as possible.

With this good news, we set out for Baladeh. The return journey was no less exciting; several snakes were sighted and a large green bullfrog made a spectacular leap over Ray's boot. We soon lost sight of Captain Ali as he hurried into the distance; but by then Ray and I were far too hot to bother so we plodded our way steadily back to Baladeh."

Back at Baladeh the rest of the team had been practising their Farsi with some success on the local children. For some unexplained reason the village girls took a strange fascination to the two girls in our team; Edith and Cherryl. Cherryl was soon bedecked with gaily coloured flowers and justly earned the name of 'flower girl.' Not to waste time the others busied themselves by making several brews of English tea and a late lunch of compo rations was consumed.

The promised eight mules were clearly not enough for all our baggage, rations and equipment. We decided to haggle again in Baladeh village for a further four. After much negotiation, we achieved some success and three sturdy animals appeared with their owners. Then began the problems of loading; each muleteer would always try to take a lighter load for his animals than that of his colleagues. Furious arguments would break out in a completely unintelligible local dialect and invariably we had to be quite forceful about the amount each mule would carry.

The decision was made that Ray and his team; Edith, John and Roger, should press on to night stop at the forest chaikhana we named 'Teahouse 1!' Ray recounts the story:

"Our three mules finally loaded, we trudged out of the village at 4pm escorted by the sergeant major. Soon we were retracing the steps of the earlier recce. The climb to the top of the first hill was only about 500 feet but, by the time they got to the top, the heat and humidity were beginning to tell. In fact the party all felt and looked as though they had walked through a shower fully dressed; little did they know that this is how they would look and feel for the next three days!

A steep descent was made on the far side of the hill to a small river which was dammed by a brick wall. The braver walked across the top of the wall while the less sure balanced gingerly on boulders which conveniently formed a line of stepping stones. At this point the countryside was very similar to a country lane in the south of England – the pathway was edged by hawthorn bushes and many other familiar deciduous trees that grow by the riverside. A short way further on the advance party reached the first of many precarious bridges. This one consisted of a series of poles and mud held together more by faith than engineering. More than one brave team member was seen to be muttering prayers as the bridge swayed and shook at each crossing! A noise which would become very familiar echoed in their ears – the roaring of a fast flowing river together with an ominous rumbling which sounded like thunder but was, in fact, huge boulders being tumbled along the river bed.

Before long the paddy fields crossed earlier in the day were reached again. This time, however, sunset was approaching and the croaking of the bull frogs began to increase in volume and threatened to break the peace of the scene. After a while the village of the gendarmerie post, which is unnamed on any map, was again reached. A welcome twenty minute break was taken at the teahouse and, for some, this was the first of many a chai drinking session. The chai is served in small glass tumblers which are supplied complete with saucer. The sugar which is added to taste is rock hard and a great deal of time is devoted to the art of chasing obstinate lumps around the bottom of the glass.

The remainder of the trek to the night stop was a steady uphill trek through the fringes of the rain forest which, to everyone's amazement, was negotiated without sighting one droplet of rain. Teahouse 1 was reached at

6.45pm and, after selecting a suitable site for the night's rest, we returned to the teahouse for refreshments. After about half an hour, the mules and muleteers appeared in the clearing before the teahouse. This was a great surprise since at Baladeh the muleteers had, despite protests, elected to take a different route to Teahouse 1, and many doubts had been cast on whether they or the kit would ever be seen again. This opinion had been reinforced when the mule train had been observed to disappear in a direction diametrically opposite to that of the advance party!"

Back at Baladeh, Sergeant Regaie erected a portable radio mast and established contact with his HQ at Kalar Dasht. He seemed a very competent operator who was capable of receiving and sending very high-speed morse. We were also impressed by the quality of the voice contact and re-assured to know that our position would be accurately plotted throughout the expedition. Meanwhile the villagers generously supplied the remainder of the team with chai and passed the tiny glasses and saucers from the window of a nearby house. The crowd gathered around us had by now grown to quite large proportions and it seemed as if all the village children had turned out to see us. Cherryl was rapidly taking on the appearance of a South Sea Island maiden with so many red and yellow flowers in her long dark hair. The men had to be content with presentations of leaves from tea bushes and other local plants.

The sunset was swiftly followed by the short twilight that is characteristic of this latitude. We viewed this with some concern and it now seemed unlikely that our mules could arrive that night and our march-in to base camp would, in consequence, be delayed. Time was critical if we were to have sufficient days on the mountain. However, just as were beginning to abandon all hope of moving, the clip-clop of mule hooves and the jangling of their bells came from the steep path above the village. Seven sturdy beasts appeared out of the gathering gloom and stood panting before us. We had hoped for eight, but it was swiftly explained that two of the mules were very strong and, for extra payment, could carry the weight of three ordinary mules. We were in no position to argue and we were anxious to get away. I rapidly agreed to this arrangement and loading commenced.

Just after 8pm we moved off in single file with Captain Ali in the lead. Soon we were again crossing the same paddy fields en route to the gendarmerie post. This time there was a difference as all the noises of a subtropical night combined to make sound effects like those of a Hollywood jungle epic – bull frogs croaked loudly, cicadas chirped incessantly and various strange unseen creatures slithered and plopped as they moved in the stagnant waters of the paddy. Every so often the darkness was broken by the curious twinkling light of glow flies that danced before us like myriads of luminous pin heads. The silhouette of Captain Ali at the lead, his automatic carbine cocked at the ready, was reminiscent of films of Vietnam jungle patrols and we all felt a strange sense of foreboding in the humid night air.

The village of the gendarmerie post was reached and we bade a few 'Salaams' to the mysterious figures who lent from balconies and were outlined against the soft glow of oil lanterns inside their wooden houses. A dog or two barked and we were obliged to circumnavigate a cow as it slept on the path before us. From the village we plunged into the forest and all the aromas of the damp woodland reached our nostrils as we stumbled along muddy tracks and across boulder strewn streams by the light of the moon and an occasional flash from our torches. By now the group had become strung out and it was often necessary to search for the fresh footprints of those in front to guide our way. At one point we paused as muffled hooves approached and swaying lanterns appeared from the darkness behind us. Fearful of bandits, we stood our ground in a small clearing and wondered if a Robin Hood style band of robbers was about to hold us to ransom. But all was well – the riders, who were friendly and only part of our mule train, had hit on the bright idea of using our two Aladdin oil lamps.

Finally at 9.45pm we emerged in a large clearing with a chaikhana on the Western side. Ray and his team were there to greet us and soon we were sipping refreshing tea inside the large teahouse building. The interior was a spacious open room with a giant-sized Samovar – or Iranian teapot – bubbling away in the corner. The muleteers were busy bedding down on long benches covered with reed matting. Captain Ali had already advised us against sleeping inside as he did not consider the benches too clean. We readily took his advice and laid our sleeping bags under the star-studded Persian night sky in the lush grass of the clearing. We had heard from mine host of the chaikhana that large black bears were common in the region and that traps had been set for them around the clearing. However, it had been a long and weary day and most of us were too tired to give another thought to the big woolly beasts that might roam our campsite.

16 June 1974

The team awoke to the sound of rushing water since a river ran by at the edge of the clearing. Such was its force that we could again hear the crashing of boulders as they were rolled along in the churning current. As the sun rose we were able to study the construction of the teahouse. It was a ramshackle wooden building with a large balcony at first floor level. The owner's family appeared to live in the upper part of the building complete with chickens and other livestock. There was an occasional glimpse of a gaily dressed woman as she busied herself with a broom of twigs. In contrast the ground floor was completely reserved for the function of tea dispensing.

The charvadars were already stirring and furiously arguing about their payment. They claimed we should pay them "must" which means money for food in addition to the amount we had agreed per mule per day. It was evident we would get nowhere by refusing their demands – as they were the only muleteers in sight, the odds were on their side. Captain Ali stepped in to ensure their price was not exorbitant. By threats of ear chopping and other dire fates, the Captain emerged from the verbal battle with a sum that was acceptable to us and grudgingly accepted by the mule men. We realised only too well the power and influence that the military wield in these remote areas and doubtless the sight of the Captain's loaded automatic deterred any muleteer from trying his luck too hard! So by 8.30am and somewhat later than planned, we were loaded up and ready to move off. This was not, however, before Roger Kelsey – our budding Lord Snowdon – had secured a group shot of the expedition aptly posed before the teahouse.

The journey through the forest that Sunday morning was quite fascinating. It surely must be one of the natural deciduous forests remaining in the world. Some of the trees were familiar to English eyes – ash, beech and a type of oak – but others were new. Their bark was often covered with green mosses and creepers; a clear indication of the normal damp climate. However, again we were blessed with good fortune and there was no sign of the rain for which the region is famed. In fact the sun shone brightly and made the forest a delightful place as pools of light penetrated the thick leaf cover to illuminate delightful green ferns. Often glades were reached which were carpeted with flowers and looked just like a clearing in English woodland. Most of us suffered pangs of homesickness at such a sight.

Teahouse 1

The mule train wound its way along the steadily climbing forest trails with a characteristic clanging of the bells tied around each animal's neck. The muleteers encouraged their mules by shouts and whistles and the sights and sounds brought thoughts of a Mexican travelogue. Ray was so moved by this scene that he was inspired to follow one mule rather too close for comfort. Rumour had it that he was recording mule noises but other theories were also voiced!

Our close contact with our beasts of burden also gave us the opportunity to study their masters. The muleteers were really a quite remarkable bunch. They appeared to vary in age from early twenties to seventy plus. Yet despite their advanced years, the older grey-haired members seemed equally agile and leapt over boulders and up mountain tracks at an astounding pace. Even more surprising were the clothes they wore. On their feet were shabby down-at-heel rubber shoes which offered little protection against the sharp rocks of the mountains. These were complemented by well-worn trousers, shirts and jackets. The older men still wore the traditional large black skull cap which had been observed by Freya Stark in her travels some 43 years earlier.

The trail crossed the turbulent white water of the mountain rivers on primitively constructed bridges. Two cantilevers of wooden poles were built out from each bank and weighted down with rocks. Frail looking lengths of timber were roped together to bridge the gap between each half. The whole structure rocked and swayed as we crossed and it was usually the case of one at a time. These bridges were characteristic of the region and we were to meet many more.

Primitive Bridge

After we had been walking for some two or more hours, the sun's heat caused most of the team to pause and refill their water bottles in one of the many small streams. This was an involved process since we were all most careful to ensure the water was correctly sterilised. However, we had been well briefed by Peter Fields, our tame hygienist, and swiftly learnt to juggle the right number of white and blue tablets.

The hot and humid conditions began to take their toll – Malcolm was beginning to lag behind the rest of the party and was evidently suffering from blisters. Fortunately, we had taken the precaution of hiring a spare mule and Malcolm was soon mounted and cantering along beside us. The only problem appeared to be that he did not know the Farsi word for 'stop' and thus had great difficulty in restraining his animal.

Later that morning the forest trees began to thin out and the trail passed through areas of open parkland type country. The views were particularly green and beautiful with long stretches of grass enclosed on two sides by the forest covered hill slopes of the broad river valley. We again crossed the Rud-e-Seh Hezar by another primitively constructed bridge and, on the far side, entered the small village of Eyndasht. The promised chaikhana did not materialise so, on the far side of the village, we sought out a shady place overlooking the river and ate a lunch consisting of anything that could be salvaged from the 24 hour compo packs issued the previous day.

The mules needed a fairly long rest for feeding and watering, so the charvadars settled themselves down to a meal of rice and eggs obtained from the nearby village. Our Iranian companions offered us some of the omelettes they were preparing but, wisely, we all stuck to our rule not to eat local food until the mountaineering phase had been completed. Captain Ali, as energetic as ever, disappeared along the river bank to try his skills at trout fishing. The rest of us stretched out lazily on the grassy bank and tried our best to escape the scorching rays of the midday sun. Whilst dozing fitfully we watched a herd of cattle crossing the bridge below in single file – a masterpiece of control by the cow hand.

It was 2pm before we were underway again. After crossing the river the route lay through an area of small green bushes which we later learnt to be wild tea. The scenery progressively became more majestic and snow-capped peaks could be seen in the far distance. At the junction of two rivers a pile of logs was found to contain a rough-hewn wooden club. Ray lost no time in demonstrating his masculine superiority by wielding the club in true 'ancient Briton' style over a cowering but defiant Cherryl.

At this point, after much examination of maps and study of the compass, we took the left-hand fork and followed a track which soon entered a small village unmarked on any of our maps. The houses were of log construction with steeply slanted wooden roofs weighted down with small boulders – evidently as a protection against the high winds and heavy snows of winter. Small groups of gaily dressed village women came to peer shyly at the passing strangers and, to the few men we saw, we bade a friendly 'Salaam Ali Khom'.

The gap between the valley slopes narrowed steadily as we moved towards our teahouse destination. Before long we were following a river which ran between forested slopes rising steeply on each side to some 3000 feet or more above the river. The path clung precariously to the side of the valley above the river banks and re-crossed the rushing torrent several times. It was here that we met the first signs of the ravages of winter – the remains of an avalanche and a snow drift; the latter not yet melted by the midday sun.

Our 'Doc', John, began to feel a little groggy; so after Malcolm had gone on for another 100 yards trying to stop his mule, they changed places. John journeyed for the rest of the day on this sturdy steed except for one rest period when Roger tried his hand at being a 'cowboy' and was nearly lost over a cliff!

The sun had almost set behind the high walls of the valley by the time we reached the second tea house at 5pm. Out crops of rock on each side of the river produced some magnificent buttresses and pinnacles and valley could be more correctly termed a gorge. Somehow the roots of forest trees still managed to cling to these steep surfaces and the thickly forested appearance remained despite the gradient.

Teahouse 2 was very small compared with the building at our first night-stop. It was little more than a log-built village house with two open-air bed boards under a small veranda. Clearly we would be obliged to sleep on the grassy banks of the river. After unloading the mules and positioning sleeping bags at strategic places, the team settled down to nightly chores. Each cooking pair prepared an evening meal from the mysteries of the compo box and sipped 'chai' served by courtesy of the teahouse keeper. The girls disappeared for an evening bathe in the river and later returned muttering that at least they were clean – unlike the rest of the party!

Meanwhile Ray and I sat around a small campfire and discussed our strategy for climbing the mountain with our Iranian colleagues – it was a leaders' council. Together we poured over both English and Iranian maps of the Elburz Range and discussed the climbing plan for the days to come. The Iranians were using military maps identical to ours but with the place names written in Arabic script. We noticed how well the Iranian team was equipped with their 'Perlon' ropes, lightweight crampons and ice axes. The Sergeant Major seemed particularly knowledgeable and had climbed the Solomon's Throne massif from Kelar Dasht on the east side on several previous occasions. However, none of the Iranians knew of the approach we had chosen and, as far as we could gather, few other climbers had ever attempted the climb by this route.

Leaders' Council

Ray and I explained our strategy and overall plan:

1   We would be climbing to 16,000 feet which could cause altitude sickness problems. We would need an acclimatisation day at Base Camp.

2   Our maps were small scale and inadequate. We had no information about climbing routes or the exact location of peaks on the massif. It would be a question of trial and error.

3   We had to leave Base on the morning of 23 June for the trek to the Valley of the Assassins. After allowing for acclimatisation we only had 3 to 4 days to achieve our objective of climbing the Solomon's Throne massif. We would therefore need a quick Alpine style assault on the mountain. This would be undertaken by Team A and backed up by Team B.

4   We would need to set up a high camp (Camp 1) on Haft Khan.

5   We would need a second summit attempt. This would be undertaken by Team C which would leave base camp a day later than Teams A & B.

6   We would need a rescue plan. Sergeant Regaie would stay in Base Camp to maintain the radio link with his HQ and with the climbing teams. Doc. John would also stay in base with Malcolm (who was the least experienced climber). The Doc. could then give medical advice via the radio link.

7   We would need strong leadership of each of the three climbing teams. We decided that Team A would be led by Mike Dawson, Team B by Ray and Team C by Peter Fields. As overall leader of the expedition I decided not to lead a summit attempt. Instead I would join Ray in Team B.

Captain Ali and his team sipped Iranian tea from their brew and generally agreed the way ahead. They made it clear that they wished to be part of the summit attempts. Captain Ali was allocated to Team A and the Sergeant Major to Team C.

Meanwhile most of the team had chosen to sleep on the river bank to the rear of the chaikhana. The outhouse was a cattle barn and they were a little hesitant about being trodden underfoot in the dead of night. However, Roger was the only one to be disturbed and he by a 'friendly' cow! The rest of us, hypnotised by the ever present roar of running water, drifted into a peaceful sleep.

17 June 1974

We awoke at 5am and ate an early breakfast. The mules were loaded after the usual arguments between muleteers as to which mules should carry the heaviest loads. However, by 7am we had left Teahouse 2 and started the ascent of the steepest part of the gorge. The forest trees completely thinned out and were replaced by sheer cliffs of rock on either side. The river rushed along the gorge bottom with tremendous momentum – often tumbling down rapids and over spectacular waterfalls in its path. The trail we were following clung precariously to the rock face on the Eastern side. We were indebted to the muleteers for their skill in controlling their well-laden animals. On many an occasion we watched with 'hearts in mouths' whilst a mule, laden with our rations and climbing gear, would balance precariously on a cliff edge hundreds of feet above the raging torrent below. But the situation would be saved by the whistles and shouts of the charvardar and the sure-footedness of the animal.

Morning Briefing

By 9am we had climbed out of the gorge and arrived at a small group of houses scarcely big enough to make up the village of Sarbalan marked on the map. Nevertheless, tea was available from one house and there was a spring of cool clear drinking water from which we could refill our water bottles. The view from here was stupendous – for the first time we could see clearly some of the high snow-capped mountains that were our ultimate objective. Haft Khan's summit was clearly visible and, to the south west, the green valley that led up to the Pass of Salambar.

We sat sipping chai and took in our surroundings. Some newly hatched ducklings swam in a small pond before us and added to the interest of the scene. Village women in black trousers and brightly covered blouses hovered in the doorways of their houses and watched us with obvious fascination. Perhaps this was not surprising as we had learnt the previous evening that we were the first Europeans to have passed by that way for a year. It was at this village that we first questioned the inhabitants about Freya Stark's visit. A village elder came forward but we drew a blank – if he did remember her visit, he was evidently scared to say so in front of our Iranian captain. Once again we noticed a fear of the military in the more remote country areas.

Several teas later and feeling much refreshed, we were once again trekking up the valley. The going was getting markedly rougher and steeper and, before long, the party had split into about four groups, each going at their own pace. The trees of the forest had now vanished and in their place were wayside hawthorns and wild rose bushes. The vivid green of the lush alpine meadows was studded with brightly coloured flowers and clusters of gentian swayed gently in the breeze. Also in evidence were several different types of birds – a plumper version of the European magpie with blue-black patches, and a type of flycatcher with bright yellow plumage.

At about 11am Doc. John complained of feeling sick and his progress became very slow. While the Sergeant Major stayed to help him along, I rushed ahead to tell the second group to catch up with the muleteers and send a mule back for the doc. I then waited for John and together we slowly trudged up the valley towards Darijan. Fortunately the others caught up with the muleteers at the village of Shahristan. Two mules and a muleteer were dispatched and these met the Doc. and I near the village of Sern. I mounted a mule to keep company with John. Not long after the last walking party had arrived we both trotted into Shahristan village on our sturdy steeds to roars of approval from the rest of the team.

Shahristan was a good opportunity to call a halt for lunch. Evidently the charvadars thought likewise for they were already beginning to unload their beasts. The lunch stop was taken at the edge of the village under the shade of a large tree. A small brook bubbled its way through the buttercup meadow where we ate our lunch and rested. Dominating this very peaceful scene were the massive crags of Haft Khan. However, we found out that the villagers did not refer to the mountain under this name – to them it was simply 'Takht-e-Sulaiman' (Solomon's Throne).

The Iranian flag fluttered proudly from a small house opposite where we sat. Our illustrious captain seized the opportunity and retrieved the flag from the roof of the building for use at our base camp. Fortunately we had taken the wise precaution of bringing a union flag with us. At least our national pride would not be injured.

At 2.15pm the expedition was underway once again. We were quite a sizeable group in all – fifteen climbers, nine muleteers and fifteen mules. John, the Doc., rode on one of the mules during this phase, the hardest part of the march-in. Soon we had by-passed Darijan, the last village on our route. The track from then on was much less well defined and only a few travellers used this route – possibly to obtain medicinal benefits from the hot springs at Ab-e-Garm. The muleteers were clearly doubtful of their chances of reaching our base camp site at Ab-e-Garm with heavy loads as there were no bridges further up the valley. However, they agreed to attempt the journey.

Before long we reached a small settlement – the last outpost of human habitation before the high mountains. Two stone built flat-roofed cottages with walls faced with mud were sited at the junction of two rivers which was aptly named 'Mian Rud' (The Middle Way). The backdrop to the cottages was the magnificent snow-capped massif of Takht-e-Sulaiman. To the left, one river led up to a large snow-filled basin which was surmounted by one of the summits of the massif. To the right, were the much nearer black and forbidding slopes of Haft Khan. The top seemed frighteningly inaccessible from where we stood some 7,500 feet below. Sandwiched between Haft Khan and a ridge further to the west, there lay a narrow steep-sided valley down which plunged the second river. This was our gateway to the mountain and the route we would take to base camp.

The journey up the valley was a precarious exercise. In places the path had slipped away and the mules were forced to take a different route from the walkers. A more difficult obstacle was the river which had to be forded at least twice on the way up. At the first crossing, Ray, Malcolm and I formed a human chain and ventured gingerly into the gushing torrent. The force was so strong we were nearly swept off our feet. Somewhat relieved we finally reached the far side and staggered on to the grassy bank com-pletely soaked. Fortunately the experience had only cost us the loss of two water bottles. Roger, Cherryl and Locky took the safer way across on the back of a mule. We had watched the muleteers crossing the river in this fashion and it was the simplest way to avoid a 'ducking'. The mules seemed remarkably sturdy despite the force of the river current.

Haft Khan's Mighty Crags

Meanwhile an advance party comprising Vic, Edi, Mike, Eddy, Pete and two of the Iranians was well ahead on the west bank of the river. There was some doubt as to the location of Ab-e-Garm, our base camp site. However, we knew it would be necessary to set up our camp on the east bank of the river so we could carry out our climbing programme without a wet start from crossing the river. Eventually, the main group caught up with the advance party and we signalled to them to join us. We watched with some trepidation as they formed a human chain and began to cross the river some 100 feet below us. However, undaunted they reached the other side and emerged with nothing more than wet feet.

By 5.20pm we reached the place pronounced by the muleteers to be Ab-e-Garm. Evidently they were correct for on the far side of the river were orange-brown stains of sulphur deposits – the location of the hot springs vividly described by Freya Stark in her book 'Valleys of the Assassins'. A few ruined stone huts and boulder circles were evidence of the popularity of the springs in days gone by.

Here we paid off the muleteers and gave them a handsome bonus for their troubles. This event gave a certain air of finality to the proceedings as we knew that once they disappeared down the valley with their animals we would be almost completely isolated from civilization with only a somewhat tenuous radio link between us and the outside world.

Our Mules ford the River

Base Camp was a truly delightful location. To the east lay the gaunt rocky face of Haft Khan's ridge, to the south the snow-capped peaks of Bamebarga and Ushgar, and to the west another lesser ridge, its top pock-marked by small snow fields. A small grassy plateau that overlooked the gushing torrent of the river below was chosen for our site. Before long we were busy pitching our tents and a semi-circle of orange arose in the peaceful valley. A squawk from behind the men was a reminder that Edith and Cherryl were still struggling to put up their Black's New Mountain tent. It was not long before someone casually remarked that the job would be much easier if they had remembered to fix the ridge pole in; for once the Girl Guides had failed!

Base Camp

Supper was cooked and afterwards some of us explored the river banks some 50 feet below. The heavy breathing on the climb back up to Base Camp was a gentle reminder that we were already operating at a height of 8,500 feet. The team would obviously need some acclimatization before the summit attempt.

However, the drama of the day was still to come. I was on an after supper stroll around the perimeter of the camp in the gathering darkness. As I entered a boulder field I placed my hand on a rock which appeared clear in the light of my torch. I immediately felt a stabbing pain in my index finger and I realised I had been bitten by a snake. As we had been told that snakes in the mountains were highly poisonous I knew I had to get to the tented area before I collapsed. I covered the 50 yards or so in record speed! I had no time to worry about my survival.

At first the team didn't believe me! But after they realised I had really been bitten there was great anxiety in the camp – I was in great pain and my throat was swelling limiting my ability to breathe. I was moved to the Doc's tent and treated for shock but I was slowly losing consciousness. I sent for Ray and handed over leadership of the expedition to him. Fortunately Doc. John was able to administer appropriate drugs to combat the pain and throat swelling. But I still spent a very groggy night suffering from the immediate after effects of the bite.

Of course we had no idea of the type of snake that had bitten me because it had been invisible in the darkness. In any case we had no anti-venom to combat any type of snake bite. Captain Ali contacted his HQ by radio and they had placed a helicopter on standby in but it could not fly in the mountains until daylight. Doc. John confided in me later that had my condition deteriorated further during the night he may have had to perform a tracheotomy operation on me so I could breathe. Even though he was a skilled RAF surgeon I didn't rate my chances of survival very high in such a remote environment.

The Snows of Ushgar

4. Solomon's Throne

18 June 1974

This was the planned altitude acclimatization day and everyone was out to make the most of the opportunity and spend a relatively leisurely day. Great anxiety continued over my condition since I was looking very ill, feeling giddy, and suffering from double vision and a badly swollen hand. My finger bore the characteristic double puncture marks of a snake bite. However, I could now breathe normally. As the day progressed I picked up a little, so it was not necessary to call in the rescue helicopter that had been placed on standby the previous evening.

At 10am Ray gave a quick briefing on the programme for the day and a flag raising ceremony was held. Both British and Iranian flags were secured to the transmitter aerial and everyone came swiftly to attention before the raised flags. Unfortunately at that moment disaster struck – one of the main guy lines of the aerial sheared and the flags fluttered to the ground; much to our chagrin.

Vic and Eddy were dispatched to recce the approaches to Haft Khan and to select a suitable route for the teams climbing to Camp 1 on the following day. The remainder set out to make improvements to the camp site. A 'loo' was constructed and aptly named 'Solomon's Throne'. Tents were also erected for the medical and food stores and a waste pit was dug.

The more venturesome made a precarious crossing of the river to explore the hot springs on the far bank. These were exactly as described by Freya Stark in her travelogue. Some way above the river bank a rock face had been transformed into a yellowish-orange colour by the chemicals in the hot spring water. Nearby two small caves had been hollowed out of the rock and, in each, rough-hewn steps led down to a small pool of tepid water which bubbled occasionally as gases escaped from a vent in the earth's interior. Each pool was at an ideal temperature for bathing and complete privacy was ensured by a wall of boulders which shielded the bather from view. Needless to say, our hot and sweaty expeditioners jumped at the opportunity for a bath and soon the lads were frolicking in the pools with much merriment. The expedition must surely go down on record as one of the cleanest ever to emerge from the mountains!

Eddy bathes in the warm spring at Ab-e-Garm

At about 3pm Vic and Eddy returned from their journey to the head of the valley. They had been able to assess the difficulty of the various approach routes to Haft Khan. All looked fairly difficult, but one ridge looked less severe and would be suitable for the next day's attempt. They seemed very impressed with the scenery they had seen – the gigantic rock mass of Haft Khan to the east, and the snow-capped peaks of Bamebarga and Ushgar to the south and west. The alpine-type flowers that abounded were equally magnificent and their reports indicated that a botanist's paradise lay ahead for the taking.

On their return the recce party had investigated a low boulder constructed building to the south of Base Camp. The building was ruined and had obviously been deserted many years ago. In the gloom of the interior an exciting find was made – several earthenware pots, almost 4 feet in height, lay in the dust. Each vessel had four carrying handles and its sides were patterned. Their origin was obscure and it was obviously a problem to be solved by skilled archaeologists. Outside, the roof of the building was covered in shards of pottery. The fragments appeared to come from the same type of vessel as had been found inside. The discovery aroused much interest in Base Camp and we were resolved to return for flashlight photography when time allowed.

Later the same afternoon a small group comprising Ali, Roger, Peter and Cherryl carried out a test of the two-way portable radio sets we had borrowed from the Special Forces detachment. They moved up river and made a check call every 15 minutes. The radios worked superbly although there was, of course, the expected break in transmission when over the 'radio horizon.'

Meanwhile, back at Base Camp there was an atmosphere of frenzied activity. The next day was to be our first attempt on the high summits and Teams A and B were checking their climbing gear and personal kit After an evening meal, most of the group retired early to bed in readiness for the early start next day. The rest sat and watched the clouds drifting up the valley below us as night fell at the little camp. From above, the impression was curiously eerie, and we felt like sailors marooned on an island in a sea of cotton wool!

Base Camp

19 June 1974

The day we had long-awaited had finally arrived. The two climbing teams were up early and ready to leave. There was an air of excitement as they stood loaded with packs, ropes and ice axes, and ready to face any challenge in the days ahead. The early morning sunlight was just creeping over the high ridge of Haft Khan and bringing pink and orange hues to the snows of Bamebarga. Team A was formed from Mike Dawson (leader), Captain Ali, Vic Last, Eddy Kemp and Locky O'Loughlin. Team B comprised Ray Condon (leader), Edi Fisher and Roger Kelsey. Regrettably I was still suffering double vision and a swollen hand from the snake bite so I couldn't take my place in Team B. Both teams were to climb independently to a high camp on Haft Khan which we would call Camp 1.

The story is now taken up by Mike Dawson:

"We left Base Camp at approximately 7am some time ahead of Team B who were to take down the mountain tents which would be required at Camp 1. The route was along a fairly well-defined path which ran roughly parallel with the river. It was very easy walking; only slightly uphill with one or two difficult parts where the path fell away to the river some hundred feet below. We continued slowly upward until the path dropped down to run alongside the river. After about 1 ½ to 2 hours walking, a snow bridge over the river was reached and we stopped for a short rest and a discussion on the route to be followed.

A high ridge could be seen some 3,000 to 4,000 feet above us with a very well-defined Haft Khan (hopefully the next camp) prominent to the left. The route selected was an obvious ridge which went almost to the summit of Haft Khan. We started up the ridge with the familiar roaring of the river ringing in our ears – a sound which was to diminish slowly during the day and could no longer be heard by early afternoon. The ridge was not easy going since there were large quantities of loose rock which called for a lot of effort to be exerted to maintain any upward movement. The ridge was a sustained slope of about 45 degrees which, although tiring to walk on, at least gave us a fairly quick height gain.

Team B, led by Ray Condon, could be seen later at the start of the ridge, at that time about 1000 feet below us. I am sure that nobody in our party would have changed places with them for 'all of the tea in

China.' Some little time later we heard shouts coming from Team B. We stopped and were somewhat surprised to see Roger Kelsey fairly close behind us, without his pack. He had discarded it temporarily in order to catch us up. He explained that Ray had fallen several times on the ascent of the loose scree and, although he was still coming up, he was now walking very slowly. We then waited while Roger returned to re-trieve his pack and the 'walking wounded' in Team B joined with us."

The events which led up to this moment are described by Ray Condon:

"Team B left Base at 6.45am with all of us carrying a hill pack weighing about 60 lbs. The slow plod up the valley started. After about 1½ to 2 hours, we left the valley by a snow bridge just above the junc-tion of two rivers and started to zig-zag up the steep mountainside. The first part of the climb followed a track made by wild goats which are common in these parts. This petered out on the lower slope and we were faced with a long three hour plod up slippery scree and a rock-strewn slope. At this stage I fell a number of times but, after taking it easy for a while, I did not suffer any long-lasting effects except for a small cut on the head where an ice axe 'jumped up at me.' By now Team A had noticed we were having problems and a short rest was taken by them whilst the two teams met up. The time was then about 1.30pm and walking had been almost continuous since Base Camp. Also by this stage, the first effects of altitude were beginning to tell – head-aches, very heavy breathing and cotton-wool knees."

Mike continues the narrative:

"The now enlarged group of eight persons then continued the slow plod-plod-plod-plod upwards. A lunch break was called by general con-sent at about 1500 feet below the ridge line of Haft Khan. The view from there took in the base camp site at Ab-e-Garm. Radio contact was made with those members of the expedition in Base and a heliograph was trained on the distant tents below. After a while the Base party acknowledged our flashes and had located us on the ridge line.

After several photographs had been taken, the combined team turned their backs on the ever widening vista around us to get back to the painful business of going upwards – after all, it was the reason why we were there! A large cluster of rocks was encountered after about *another two hours walking and, as everyone was fairly tired and the ridge was becoming more rocky, we decided to set up Camp 1 at the rocks. We had now reached a height of 13,900 feet.*

We made several brews before looking for suitable sites for the tents. As there was no level ground at all, it was necessary to hew out tent-size level platforms out of the ridge. Everyone found this very tiring, the altitude being a great handicap to any form of physical labour. Even so, Vic Last was rumoured to have lowered the mountain by ten feet or so!

Camp 1

After the tents had been erected a meal of Vestas was cooked by all; the only non-participant being Edi who had emerged from her tent earlier only to be sick. She now re-appeared and, after a hot orange drink, pronounced herself much better. Eddy Kemp was also suffering with a severe headache, almost certainly due to the altitude, and Roger Kelsey was troubled with diarrhoea!

Everybody turned in fairly early after looking at the sun going down over the numerous mountains that we could now see. The river was now a mere silver line a long way below us with the snow bridge just a white dot."

Meanwhile, back at Base the seven remaining members were on rescue standby in case of emergencies with the climbing teams. Sergeant Regaie kept a regular radio watch with his HQ and John Dove operated the portable radio link with Team A. A position report was received from the climbing teams every 1 to 2 hours. Most of the Base party spent a fairly quiet day – that is with the exception of John and I who crossed the river to bathe in the hot springs on the opposite side. John also collected some rock specimens there. Having achieved our objective, we had great difficulty re-crossing the river and, in the end, we were hauled out very much wetter than we started by Peter and Malcolm.

That evening we gathered around the radio to listen to the events at Camp 1. On hearing of the sickness problems the climbing teams were encountering, John cancelled the trial of a drug called Lucidrill that we had been taking to improve energy. He told all participants not to take any more of the drug. He also passed medical advice to those at Camp 1 who were suffering from ailments. Shortly afterwards the Base party were somewhat alarmed to see that the two Iranians were furiously digging deep channels around their tents. They guessed a deluge was likely and, in a session of frenzied activity, copied their example for their own tents. However, the rain when it did fall during the night was not too torrential and quickly drained away.

20 June 1974

The principal activities of the day were to climb Alam Kuh, the highest peak of the massif, and for Team C (comprising Sergeant Major Zamanpour, Peter and Cherryl) to climb from Base Camp to Camp 1. Team A had been chosen for the summit attempt and Mike Dawson describes the experiences of the climb:

"The day started with a shaking tent and the muffled sound of 'Come on; it's a quarter to five!' We peered from the tent door to see a terrific

view in the cold grey early morning light. There was a very blustery wind blowing, so duvets were the order of the day whilst we brewed a quick tea and munched a couple of oatmeal blocks. Three of us were up and about: Locky, Vic and myself. Eddy had decided not to come with us as his headache was still troubling him. We wasted no time in getting Captain Ali out as well and our summit party was complete. The only other sign of life that early was a peculiar circular object with grey and black stubble on it protruding from one of the other tents. A strange groaning noise was issuing from it punctuated by long pauses. After a careful approach we came to the conclusion that this must be none other than Ray carrying out a radio check with Base!

I took over the radio call from Ray and spoke to Base letting them know the state of the party, our route and so on. The radio call delayed our start somewhat so we left at about 6.10am. The climb initially was up some very large rock boulders. Most of these were solid and great care was necessary to avoid twisting ankles or legs. The angle of the climb was quite steep and snow lay between the boulders. However, it was a quick method of gaining height and was infinitely preferable to the monotonous plod of the previous day. This terrain continued until a small snowfield was reached at the top of the ridge. All members carefully crossed the snow with the aid of their ice axes. On the far side we were back on fairly loose rock which we traversed up and to the right. After only half an hour we had reached the top of the Haft Khan ridge.

The view from this point was absolutely breathtaking! We could see that the Solomon's Throne massif was in the form of a horseshoe with several peaks – the highest of which was Alum Kuh (16,000 feet). The ridge we were on was one arm with the opening of the horseshoe to our left behind us. The summit of Alam Kuh was about two thirds of the way around the horseshoe and was only about 800 feet above us. Between us and the summit was only about half a mile horizontally. However, that distance included a large snow bowl which fell away from us for about 2500 feet to a small ice pool at the bottom and then swept up steeply on the other side. At the top of the far ridge the snow slope was corniced along its length with an almost vertical 1000 feet drop below.

The ridge itself was very narrow right at the top with the loose rock we had ascended on its gentler side. Even this fell away fairly steeply for about 1000 feet before it became the gentler ridges of our Camp 1. Along the length of the ridge were several minor peaks rising, on average, some 200 feet above the ridge line. As the time was only 10.30am we certainly seemed to be in with a very good chance for Alam Kuh. As we moved along the ridge line towards the summit, it became obvious that the route was going to involve a lot more climbing than we had initially anticipated. We stopped at about 11.30am just below one peak at a spot which afforded us our best view of the ridge yet. From where we stood, it was apparent that the ridge dropped considerably – certainly some 300 to 400 feet – and then climbed up to the first of several rock walls. It was difficult to judge the severity, but at 15000 feet with 2000 feet exposure, I don't think any of us was very keen. Even with the best climbing gear, the time factor would still have precluded an ascent and a return to Camp 1 in the same day.

Solomon's Throne

I had been sitting and talking with Captain Ali whilst viewing all this and, on going back to see Locky and Vic for their comments, I found Locky, with his rucksack still on, fast asleep! We decided that we would scale one of the lesser peaks along the ridge and chose one which the

Iranians called Korman (or Kaman). This had a height of about 15,200 feet which is not far below the height of Mont Blanc. We climbed the peak and took many photographs including the full panorama of the majestic Solomon's Throne. Both Vic and I took full 360 degree shots from where we were.

We descended by the same route we had come up and stopped just below Haft Khan for a brew and a bite to eat. It was at this rest stop that I was overtaken by the dreaded altitude headache. However, after a tea and an Aspirin it soon disappeared. The descent was very carefully negotiated – particularly through the boulder fields. Even so, we stopped several times to admire the view and just to 'soak up' the mountains. We came in sight of Camp 1 in the late afternoon after experiencing one slight mishap when Vic did his best to sever a tendon in his foot – fortunately unsuccessfully.

Korman Conquered

The arrival in Camp 1 was of a slightly disappointed team, although Edi's tea did a lot to revive spirits. It was then the usual round of Vestas and a chat before turning in for an early night."

Back at Camp 1, Team B had kept a careful watch throughout the day for Team C which was aiming to join the Camp 1 group for a second summit attempt the next day. As has been recounted, the summit party (Team A) returned to Camp 1 at 3.30pm after a very hard day. Despite the disappointment of not reaching Alam Kuh, Team B was delighted to hear that they had reached an estimated 15,200 feet and the good news was passed to Base Camp at the next radio call.

By 5pm the Camp 1 group were becoming concerned that Team C had not yet been seen. Unfortunately, it had not been possible to equip them with a radio, but everyone was confident that the Sergeant Major, a very experienced climber, would have contacted either Camp 1 or Base Camp had an emergency arisen. The ridges up to Camp 1 were such that even at 200 yards a small camp could easily be lost from view in the dead ground. Small search parties were sent out to scour the ridges further up the valley in case Team C had chosen a route up another spur. However, there was still no sign of the missing team and, as darkness was approaching, it was agreed that no action would be taken until morning.

The last radio call of the day was made at 7pm. It was agreed with Base that no further group would attempt the summit until Team C had been found. It was also decided that Roger, who was still unwell, and Mike who was suffering from painful toe nails bruised on an earlier climb, would both descend to Base Camp on the following day.

Down at Base Camp the events of the day had been somewhat different. Team C had left for Camp 1 at about 6am. I was feeling much better and my double vision had gone. Doc John pronounced me fit enough to climb. I elected to attempt the ridge to the west of Base Camp. For my companion, Malcolm, this would be his first experience of a high mountain climb. Here is my account of the climb:

> "The first problem was to cross the river but, just as we were about to ford the rushing torrent, some nomad tribesmen appeared and constructed a primitive bridge of two logs weighted down by rocks. We added to the safety of this and provided a hand line by stretching a 120 feet climbing rope across the gap and securing the ends to large boulders on each side.
>
> Doc John and Sergeant Regaie had been left in Base to operate the radio link whilst the function of the rescue party had been taken on by Team B at Camp 1. We waved farewell to the two in Base from the far

bank of the river and began the climb of a steep grassy ridge. At first the ascent was relatively easy though extremely steep and we were obliged to zig-zag to gain height without too much exhaustion. After three hours of steady climbing up a long ridge, we encountered several large rock outcrops and buttresses which had to be very carefully negotiated. By now we were up to the snow line at about 11,000 feet and several small snowfields had to be crossed or skirted around. Our ice axes proved very useful for this manoeuvre.

Although we were both fairly exhausted and beginning to feel the effects of altitude, a determined push took us to the top of the ridge line by 1pm. We sat down to have lunch and admire the view which was stupendous. From our 12,000 feet vantage point we could see the complete Haft Khan ridge on the opposite side of the valley and, beyond that, the high summit of Alam Kuh. To the south, looking up the valley, the magnificent snow-covered horseshoe of Gamaura was crystal clear in the bright sunlight. We could even distinguish the tiny orange specks that were Camp 1 on the steep side of Haft Khan across the valley.

We had arranged to make a heliograph signal to Doc John from the top of the ridge. Unfortunately, our attempt was thwarted by the sun's position and we could not reflect downwards into the valley below. Instead we decided to climb a small peak which capped the ridge immediately behind where we sat. This peak juts up some 500 feet above the ridge line and was unmarked and unnamed on any of our maps. After a further hour we had reached the rocky summit and looked down a sheer precipice on the west side where the mountain drops vertically some several thousand feet into the Alamut Valley.

This was our first view of the legendary valley – the home of the Assassins during the Middle Ages and the place which held a curious fascination in the minds of all the team. From where we stood we could see the green of the Valley floor but a heat haze obscured the view down the Valley to Garmarud and other villages the expedition would later visit. However, the surrounding mountains were breathtaking in their beauty with snow-capped peaks to the east, west and south, and the barren rock peak of Narghiz-Kuh along the ridge to the north-west. So impressed was Malcolm with his first 'alpine-style' peak that we *elected, unofficially, to name the peak we had climbed as 'Simbla-Kuh' from a combination of our names.*

We made a rapid descent to Base Camp via a different route and two rather weary expeditioners arrived back by 6pm. There we found Doc John who was becoming a little concerned for our safety, particularly as he had not seen the pre-arranged heliograph flash. More worrying was the lack of news of Team C, but there was little that could be done with darkness descending fast on the Camp. The Base party retired to a somewhat restless night hoping that the next day would bring better tidings."

21 June 1974

The immediate concern was the safety of Team C and, at an early morning radio call between Camp 1 and Base Camp, we decided to send out search parties from both locations. At Camp 1 a fairly good night's sleep had been had by all. Even the tunnel tents stayed dry and there were none of the condensation problems we had previously experienced when using them at lower altitudes. An early start was made by some. Edi, however, felt unwell at first, but fortunately her headache soon passed off. Mike and Roger left for Base at 9am and the remainder of Camp 1 searched the nearby ridges and maintained a listening watch on their radio for news of Team C. Eventually at 3pm the message came through that all was well – Mike and Roger had reached Base Camp and Peter, of Team C, had met Bruce with the news that the rest of his team were safe and descending slowly to Base.

The Camp 1 group then decided that, as a descent to Base was planned for the next day in any case, there was little to be gained from spending another night at altitude. A high speed return to Base would be made and, if it was impossible to reach the river by nightfall, an intermediate camp would be set up. Camp 1 was struck in record time and the descent was started at 3.45pm. The river was reached by 5.15pm – a record perhaps (but not many people have tried it!). The journey back along the river bank was also completed at a rapid pace and Base Camp was reached by 6.20pm giving an elapsed time for the descent of 6400 feet of 2 hours 35 minutes!

Meanwhile Malcolm and I had left Base Camp early that morning to journey up to the head of the valley where we would station ourselves at strategic points and scan the horizon with binoculars in search of the missing Team C. Two key points were chosen near the snow bridge above the river junction and then came the tedious task of waiting, watching and hoping. Whilst engaged in this task we spotted a mountain eagle of brownish plumage and a very large wingspan being pursued by ten or more ravens. The eagle had probably attacked their young for they were pursuing the giant bird noisily but to no avail. We also watched several small birds and one, with pink feathers, was particularly colourful.

At 12.30pm Roger and Mike appeared at the snow bridge after a steep and painful descent from Camp 1. Just after they had departed over the horizon for Base Camp, a sunburnt bearded figure was observed descending the slope above the snow bridge at some considerable speed. From a distance it appeared as if the Sergeant Major was returning with news of Team C, but no, it was none other than Peter Fields. He takes up the story of the missing Team C:

"We left Base at Ab-e-Garm at 6am on 20 June and, after a walk of about 1½ hours, we left the main track and commenced the climb of Haft Khan. The climb was extremely long and, with heavy packs, proved to be very strenuous. However, the Team continued plodding up the mountain until approximately 3pm. By then, the Sergeant Major was well ahead. This was probably because due to the difference in his physical capacity compared with the other two members and he was obviously far more used to operating at high altitudes, and found it difficult to maintain a slower pace than normal.

The Team carried on until sheer exhaustion forced us to camp for the night on a ridge to the west of Haft Khan at approximately 14,900 feet. We had not seen any sign of Camp 1 or the other two teams and we could only assume we had reached a different part of the ridge. We set up a new camp (Camp 1*) at the top of a snow-field on the leeward side of the ridge. Cherryl was sick and looking very pale, possibly through exhaustion, but equally due to the effects of high altitude. I was also suffering from slight nausea, but other than that had no ill effects.

Early next morning we carried out a recce along the ridge to the east and west in the hope of meeting the other teams. We were unsuccessful and decided that the best plan was to return to Base as soon as possible to avoid an emergency rescue operation by the rest of the expedition. The Sergeant Major had left earlier on a route back to Base

Camp via the ridge line where he hoped to locate Captain Ali and the others. Cherryl was still feeling ill and so a very slow descent was made for the first third of the downward journey. I then decided I should go ahead as fast as possible to obtain assistance for Cherryl and to notify Base Camp of our whereabouts.

I reached Bruce at the snow bridge at 12.55pm. After a short discussion, he went up the mountain to help Cherryl whilst I continued to Base Camp in company with Malcolm. Once there, we made an immediate radio call to notify Camp 1 of Team C's safety."

Meanwhile Cherryl had slid down a scree slope and had finally come to rest at the top of a snow gully. The snow gully started about 1000 feet up from the river and continued almost down to the valley bottom. Having decided that the scree was as dangerous as the snow, Cherryl chose the latter and attempted to glissade down the slope – unfortunately in a sitting-down position. Having nearly reached the bottom of the slope, a duvet fell from her rucksack and the tackle to retrieve it ended up with Cherryl sprawled on top of the duvet with the rucksack on top of her! Fortunately I located her five minutes later and carried her rucksack back to Base. On the way we met Doc John and Malcolm who had returned to give any assistance that may have been needed. Base Camp was reached at 6pm. In the meantime the Sergeant Major had returned safely back to Base after a very long trek along the ridge. Although Team C had had an experience that could have proved dangerous, they did have the consolation of having reached a height of 14,900 feet without too much trouble.

That day at Base our Doc had been visited by a travelling Iranian doctor who clutched an Iran Air bag containing hypodermic syringes – his medical kit for the remote villages. Apparently he and Doc John had spent a while swapping notes!

The day concluded with a minor op by our Doc. Poor Mike had his toe nails removed but fortunately he stayed cheerful in the 'open-air theatre' and even insisted on photographing the event! However, their removal would pose us a problem as he would be unable to wear boots for the next few days, and would therefore need transporting during the walk out to Shahrak – our bus rendezvous.

22 June 1974

After so much activity and excitement we were glad of the opportunity to spend a fairly quiet day in Base preparing for the march-out on the next day. For most of the expedition it was a chance to meditate on what had been achieved and to hear the stories of each climbing team.

Jubilant Group

Captain Ali had sent a message to the nearest village, Darijan, to say that we wished to negotiate the hire of mules for our journey out. During the morning a wizened old man in a battered brown trilby and shabby suit arrived by mule at Base Camp. He announced himself to be the headman of Darijan and that he had come to represent the muleteers of his village.

As is customary in the Middle East, tea was prepared and we sat crossed-legged in a circle to begin the lengthy negotiations for hire of the mules. We listened fascinated to the haggling as Captain Ali put forward our requirements and terms, and the headman gave counter arguments to obtain the best price for his muleteers. All this went on in an incomprehensible babble of Farsi with voices being raised to shouting pitch at times. We came to the conclusion that nothing was settled quickly in those parts.

After a translation by the Captain, it transpired that one of the muleteers we had hired for the march-in to Base had spread word around Darijan that we were bad men who had not paid them their wages. We were flabbergasted – nothing could be further from the truth! However, the malicious rumour did mean that the muleteers would not come from Darijan unless we paid them in advance for the three day journey to Shahrak.

A price was finally agreed and Ray somewhat reluctantly parted with the advance payment; it being evident that we would get nowhere until they saw the 'colour of our money.' The muleteers had a complete monopoly over us – there were no other mules within miles and they knew it. Even so, we did wonder whether we had just been taken for the best con-trick of all time, and if we would ever set eyes on the little wizened old man or our money again!

We took the opportunity to question the visiting headman on his recollections of Freya Stark's visit. He was unable to help us as he had lived Tehran at the time and had been sent to Darijan since then by the Government. However, on hearing the story of my snake bite, he explained that there are only two types of dangerous snake in the mountains. From a description of the bite I had received he named the snake 'Ayi' and explained that without medical aid such a bite would normally prove extremely serious and perhaps even fatal. At this news I was beginning to look a 'little green around the gills.' All the while the tape on the recorder was turning slowly and we had obtained an interesting conversation for further study on our return to Akrotiri.

The principal activities of the day were baths in the hot springs and dhobying of our sweat-stained mountain clothes. The wash process was quite a ritual and was undertaken in age-old style by plunging the clothes in the ice cold water of the river and then rub-a-dubbing them on a suitable flat stone. After a while the river bank took on the appearance of a Chinese laundry with colourful garments laid out on boulders in the hot sun.

A diversion was created by Mike who, although he was still suffering from his toe-nail amputations, could not bear the thought of missing a bath. We hit on the bright idea of trussing up his feet in thick polythene sheet so that his bandages could be kept dry. He looked quite a picture as he hobbled around with an enormous parcel on each leg!

The highlight of the day was the catching of a snake by Captain Ali. We heard a shout from some village boys who had spotted a snake in the rocks on the far side of the river. The Captain tracked it down and managed to pin it to the ground with a forked stick. This way the reptile's head was trapped and he was able to bring the wriggling silver-brown snake back to Base Camp. Everyone gathered around the great hunter and studied the snake with interest. It was about 2½ feet long and was probably the same type that had bitten me. The Sergeant Major, who seemed very knowledgeable about snakes, showed us how to sever the snake's fangs to make it harmless. Eventually, the Iranians killed the snake, and the Doc amused himself by dissecting the reptile and mounting the skin on a pole. Regrettably, this trophy was lost in transit the following day and could not take its place of honour on the Club Room wall at Akrotiri.

Sergeant Major's Snake

During the afternoon, Malcolm and I journeyed to the head of the river to collect specimens of some of the beautiful wild flowers that abounded. Purple and yellow irises provided a tinge of exotic colour to the lush green alpine meadows and, in other places, there were fields of forget-me-nots, harebells and buttercups. A white flower similar to Eidelweiss carpeted the ground. There were also indigenous flowers of a type and form strange to European eyes. So great was the variety of flowers that some 50 to 60 species were collected and pressed during the space of four hours. The walk was also a good opportunity to study the insect life that was attracted by so many flowers. There were butterflies similar to the more familiar

Swallowtails, Red Admirals and Painted Ladies of the English countryside. Large brown spiders with white-spotted backs clung to their webs stretched between the slender flower stems. Several types of locust and beetle were also observed.

Another interesting spectacle was the arrival at Chai Barengan, the ruined teahouse just below the snow bridge, of a group of nomads who had come from the south to seek summer pastures in the high alpine meadows. They had erected a large marquee-size tent on one of the meadows as their living quarters. On the surrounding hillsides were scattered several hundred animals; mainly goats and sheep but including a few cows. Malcolm and I stayed a while to study this colourful scene before returning to Base.

Meanwhile Edi and Cherryl had explored down river and had located a superb waterfall. The day concluded with a packing-up session in readiness for the next day's journey. Everyone retired for an early night.

5.   Valley of the Assassins

23 June 1974

The day began at 5am and, after a quick breakfast, the tents were taken down and the equipment was finally packed in readiness for the journey. We were somewhat surprised to see the first of the mules appear on the skyline at 6.30am – our faith in human nature was restored! The kit was soon loaded and the expedition assembled for group photographs before departure. This was the time for saying our own personal farewell to the beautiful valley that had been our home for the last few days. It was not a place any of us would ever forget.

We started down the path to Darijan at 7.45am. Both Mike and Roger were mounted on mules because the former could not walk and Roger was still very weak from his stomach trouble. As he was unable to wear boots, Mike sat aside his steed resplendent in his bright red climbing socks and swiftly acquired the name 'Donkey Dawson.' Roger's 'ding-a-ling' hat tinkled with every mule step. Despite the endless patience of the animals, both riders had difficulty staying on their backs for the first mile.

The long procession of mules, men and the two girls wound its way down the narrow and treacherous path. Seven of the team forded the river very early on whilst the rest were content to let the mules take them across further down. The process of riding mule-back through the torrent needed some acrobatic skill and great amusement was caused by Malcolm, who mounted and promptly slipped backwards off his mule, and by me – I made the crossing spread-eagled across my mule's rear and hanging on for dear life!

While we were performing such antics Captain Ali had caught and killed another snake. We certainly voted him the big hunter and hero of the trip. Using his technique, the capture of the reptile seemed so simple, yet we were sure that anyone without his skill would have rapidly met a dire fate.

We reached Mianrud after studying some of the magnificent rock buttresses which led up to Haft Khan from the entrance to the valley. Our thoughts turned to the possibilities of a future expedition merely to attempt the climb of these stupendous crags which stretched skywards up the great gaunt mass of the mountain's western face. Nothing could be nearer to a climber's paradise!

As the Doc, Ray and I passed the cottages at Mianrud we discovered that one outwardly normal wall was, in fact, a honey-comb and the home of a swarm of bees. Doc John succeeded in getting stung but, fortunately, he was not allergic to the insects and did not suffer greatly.

We moved on through bright green meadows and the purple patchwork-quilt landscape near Darijan. As we came into the outskirts of the village, the advance party were gathered around a young Iranian girl of about seven who had lost her little toe in a rock fall a week before. The girl's father was very anxious for her well-being and asked Doc John to examine her wound. The young lass very bravely permitted Peter Fields to undo the rough dressing and to clean her foot in the water of a small stream. The wound was looking ugly and the bone had been laid bare.

Doc John's experience as a surgeon came to the fore and he swiftly diagnosed that only hospital treatment and the complete removal of the damaged bone would effect a cure and prevent gangrene from setting-in. The nearest hospital was three day's mule ride away and it seemed doubtful whether the girl's father would make the journey, particularly as daughters are not held in the same high esteem as sons in Muslim countries. Nevertheless, he was sufficiently concerned to follow the expedition for several miles to our lunch stop later in the day. There, Doc John unloaded the medical bag from a mule and gave him antibiotics to relieve his daughter's suffering.

At Darijan some of us visited an ancient watermill. In a low mud-roofed building an 'old crone' stood guard over a primitively constructed wheel which spun around noisily as it was driven by a bucket scoop in the river below. We paused for a photograph of this strange building and its custodian.

After Darijan the expedition descended steeply into Sern where our passage through the village was watched by almost all the residents as they stood on the flat mud roofs of their houses and waved. At times like these we almost felt like royalty in a State procession!

We crossed the river by a rickety log bridge and, after passing through a herd of goats and sheep, began the steep trudge up the slope on the far side. The sun was now high in the sky and its rays were beating down unmercifully upon us. By the time we reached the top, some 2000 feet higher up, we were sweating profusely and suffering from an advanced stage of exhaustion. It had not helped when one of the mules had bolted throwing those nearby into the wayside thorn bushes!

Some consolation was gained from the view. From where we stood at the top of the spur between the two main branches of the Rud-e-Seh Hezar, we could look back on the now familiar skyline of the Solomon's Throne Massif. We paused to gaze at the spectacular panorama and to use our cameras to advantage.

The next part of the journey was a long trail which wound down the side of the spur and eventually reached the village of Maran after crossing the western branch of the river. Maran itself is a large village of flat-roofed mud-walled houses, which appear to be balanced one above the other on the steep mountainside. A white domed building stood out in the centre of a cluster of houses and poplar trees. Captain Ali thought this was a mosque or tomb constructed in memory of a man who first founded the village.

We stopped for lunch under a giant walnut tree. From the size of its trunk it must have been there several hundred years – and possibly even outdated the village. Some colourfully dressed children stood shyly watching us. They gathered more confidence when we threw them a few compo sweets. These they seemed to relish and were soon back with outstretched hands waiting for more.

At 2.30pm we were once again on the trail and began the long steady haul up to the Pass of Salambar. The scenery steadily changed and, at each new turn of the track, a completely new vista was revealed. Our route passed along the edge of a miniature Grand Canyon – a stupendous gorge with sheer rock walls almost 2000 feet deep. As we gained height we were following the river to its source near the top of the pass. The water still flowed with tremendous force and at one point we forded the river gingerly on stepping stones just above a roaring waterfall.

Before long we had left the hedgerows and wayside hawthorns of the valley and emerged on a grassy hill slope which rose steeply to the Pass. It was a steady climb as we followed the zig-zag trail up the slope. On the way up someone noticed a deadly black scorpion scuttle across the path. This caused some alarm as we were well aware of the dangers of a sting from one of these insects. However, as the time was now 4.30pm and we had reached a height of nearly 10,000 feet, we decided to risk the scorpions and spend a night under the stars before attempting the crossing of the Pass.

We chose a site for Camp 2 near a bubbling spring – the source of the river we had followed for so many miles. I briefed everyone on the dangers from black scorpions and the need to shake out boots and other likely places they may choose. The muleteers unloaded their animals and the expedition settled down to the task of preparing an evening meal. Sleeping bags were stretched out on the short turf and it was not long before they were filled with weary bodies.

We had been told earlier by a young lad from the small settlement of Salambar that wolves and bears were fairly common on the hillside. So we spent the night rather uneasily wondering what possible perils would befall us. However, the danger did not come from scorpions, wolves or bears but from our four-legged beasts of burden and their masters. To recount the story:

> "During the night I was awakened by a thudding of hooves and awoke to see a stray mule trotting straight towards Ray's sleeping bag. A shout brought Ray to his senses and he rolled out of the way just in time! Just as I was drifting to sleep again a yellow light and crackling sound caused me to sit bolt upright. A Batman shaped figure stood menacingly before me and was silhouetted against the flames of a blazing thorn bush. For a fleeting moment I thought I had met my doom! I then realised that the figure was merely a muleteer who was feeling the cold and had set light to a bush for warmth! His strange shape was produced by the square cape of felt he was wearing. These capes, called 'shulars,' are popular with the muleteers and are worn tied in two shoulder knots or with comic stumps of dummy sleeves."

24 June 1974

After loading the mules, we moved off at 6.45am and took an hour to reach the top of the Salambar Pass at a height of 11,500 feet. A few isolated snow patches remained, but the path we took across the top was completely clear. We had now reached the highest point on the walk out and, from now on much to our relief, the journey would be mainly downhill.

At the top was a small plateau which was dotted with small cacti and a type of everlasting flower which looked like crisp yellow paper. A ruined teahouse lay to the west side of the path and it appeared unchanged since Freya Stark had described it in her travels. Apparently, it had been destroyed by heavy snowfalls in 1930.

From where we stood we were able to look back for the last time at Solomon's Throne. At that time our thoughts cannot have been very different – the mountain had made a permanent impression on all of us. There was also a beautiful panorama to the south – on the opposite side of the Alamut Valley lay the snow-capped peaks of the Sat Mountain and Shah Elburz; their summits some 2000 feet higher than Salambar Pass.

The descent on the far side of the Pass was at first very gradual. We crossed lush green meadow pastures to the village of Pichuban. At Pichuban, the usual crowd of villagers watched us pass. Some of the team were lucky enough to observe a local custom. As they passed through the village they saw a house with three pairs of shoes pointing towards the door. Apparently this meant that a young man of the village had asked for the hand in marriage of a girl from that house.

After Pichuban, we crossed a much drier and sandier terrain than we had seen during the expedition so far. It was evident we were entering the steppe region on the south side of the central ridge of the Elburz – an area where the rainfall is, like Cyprus, very sparse.

The area was infested with grasshoppers. There were many brightly-coloured red, green and orange species that hopped across the path in all directions – for a collector of such insects it would have been a paradise. We also noticed snake trails in the dry sandy soil and found a snake skin that had been shed.

Soon we were going down into the Alamut itself. Here at last was the legendary valley which held a special magic for us all. In the early Middle Ages this remote and naturally well-protected valley had been the mountain stronghold of a branch of the Ismaili sect of the Shi'a Muslims. Led by Hassan-i-Sabbah the 'Hashishins', as his followers were called, practised their vile and murderous acts as far afield as the Syrian coast – hence the adoption by the Crusaders of the name 'assassin' and its subsequent appearance in the English language of today.

The Assassins constructed a number of castles in the Alamut. One castle lay at each end of the valley and a third, the headquarters castle, was built on top of the imposing Rock of Alamut. From these castles the Assassins ruled over their domain for 150 years. The Assassins were overrun in 1256 by Hulague Khan's mongol hordes who invaded Persia from the east and the population of the valley was massacred. Hulague Khan was the grandson of the legendary Ghenghis Khan. Although the mongols destroyed the castles, we hoped that sufficient ruins would remain to bear witness to the Assassins' occupation of the valley.

Mule Train 'neath the Waterfall

As we looked down into the Alamut, we could see the thin green strip of fertile cultivation that marked the Alamut Rud. The rocks on the far side of the valley were now a reddish colour in contrast to the blacks and greys of Solomon's Throne. Between us and the river below lay some of the most rugged rocks we had ever seen. Gigantic blocks of granite had been tumbled one on top of the other to form a scene which was awe-inspiring in its scale.

The path down through this 'land of the giants' hung precariously from the rock face and, in some places, it was so steep that the mules slipped and stumbled – one animal slipping completely over and needing assistance to get to its feet. Needless to say, Mike and Roger had one of the most frightening journeys of their lives and both were instantly ready to jump should their animal slip down a precipice. Fortunately all was well and they survived the journey with only a few grey hairs to show for it.

At one point on the steep descent the path passed under a small waterfall which tumbled from the overhang above. It was a fascinating experience to see a miniature rainbow reflected in the falling water. We remembered that Freya Stark had mentioned the very same waterfall in her book. Another interesting feature of the descent was the giant lizards we spotted basking in the sun on wayside boulders. These brown scaly reptiles were up to two feet long and looked like tiny dragons as they scuttled out of our way.

We reached the large village of Garmarud in time for lunch. Garmarud is pleasantly situated in the fast flowing Alamut Rud just below where the river passes through a spectacular gorge. It is a natural gateway to the valley and we realised why Hassan's followers had chosen to site their castle 'Nevisar Shah' on the rock buttresses which arose precipitously behind the village.

We chose to lunch stop on the south side of Alamut Rud which we crossed by means of a very long and rickety log bridge of the usual type. It was evidently not too strong, for when 'Donkey Dawson' appeared on his mount a small village boy ran across the bridge to him gesticulating wildly that he must dismount before attempting the crossing!

We sat in the long grass under walnut, plane and poplar trees and discussed a plan of campaign. Two objectives remained for the expedition – to climb and photograph the Rock of Alamut; and to interview the elders of Garmarud on their recollections of the stay of Freya Stark in their village. It was clear that we could not achieve both targets within the time available unless we split forces. An advance party of five to be led by Vic Last would leave after lunch for the journey down the valley. They would set up camp at a location from where they could launch an attempt on the Rock of Alamut early the next morning. The remainder of the team would stay in Garmarud overnight and carry out the Freya Stark project research.

Garmarud Backdrop

I discussed the plan with Captain Ali. At first he was somewhat hesitant as none of the Iranians, either the Special Forces or the muleteers, were happy to venture down the valley during the late afternoon or evening. The problem was that the area below Garmarud was still malarial and Iranians did not have the benefit of the protection given to us by the Paludrine tablets we took daily. The Captain feared for the safety of the advance party without any army protection. However, he eventually agreed to a compromise whereby he wrote a note in Farsi explaining the group's presence and that he, a Captain in His Imperial Majesty's army, was responsible for their safekeeping. It was also agreed that the advance party would use the portable radios to maintain contact with the team at Garmarud.

After lunch the advance party set off at a cracking pace with Vic in the lead. We waved them farewell and wished them success on their assault on the Rock. Those who remained at Garmarud were soon besieged by young boys who offered to fetch us fresh water and wild cherries and to wash our clothes in the river. They were very persistent and their numbers grew steadily. Eventually Sergeant Regaie spoke to them in Farsi. Whatever he said must have had the right effect for they scampered into the distance. As we rested on the grass beneath the trees, we gazed in amazement at the incredible jumbled mass of volcanic rock which formed a back drop to the village. The rock face had weathered into a tremendous variety of over-hangs, fissures and chimneys and the opportunities for climbing were endless. Most of us mentally worked out how we could tackle each likely route.

Meanwhile the Captain had arranged for Doc John, Ray and I to meet the village elders at 5pm. We gathered around the tea glasses as several bent old men walked slowly towards us. Our interview proved most profitable. Our visitors included a younger man who turned out to be the son of the now deceased muleteer who had guided Freya Stark on her travels. Also present was a former village headman who remembered Freya Stark's visit very well.

Our interview technique was simple but effective. Doc John and I posed questions which were interpreted by Captain Ali, whilst Ray furiously manipulated the controls of his cassette recorder to obtain a 'historic' sound track of the interview. All the while we sipped chai and helped ourselves to cherries from a large bowl in the centre of the circle. The cherries were small, light-pink coloured and slightly bitter. We copied the local style of eating by dipping each cherry in salt. Apparently this avoided the staining of the teeth which the juice of this fruit can produce.

We learnt about several interesting facets of local life from our ques-tions. Since the time of Freya Stark's visit the Iranian Government had introduced several changes which had benefitted the villagers. For example there were greater opportunities for education and a fine village school had now been built. Schemes existed for eradicating the malarial mosquito and for providing agricultural advice and assistance. The style of dress had been compulsorily changed by the late Shah and the younger men wore European clothes. Even the older men had rejected the knee length breeches which were characteristic of the region in 1931.

Elders' Interview

Once the villagers knew that John was a doctor a number of medical questions were posed. The former headman who had proved so helpful needed advice for his 'gall stones.' The strangest case was an elderly bandy-legged muleteer who claimed he was suffering from a foot complaint which Doc John swiftly diagnosed as 'athlete's foot.' Quite rightly, he refused to give treatment unless the patient first washed his filthy and mud stained feet in the river. Evidently such action was quite beyond the comprehension of the muleteer who had probably never washed them in his life. The next thing we knew he was following the traditional remedy of placing his feet in a bowl of mule dung!

We concluded our interview by asking if we could see the house where Freya Stark had stayed. We crossed the river and entered the main part of the village. After crossing the flat mud roofs of several houses, we reached the small house where Freya Stark had stayed some 35 years before. We removed our shoes and stooped to enter through a low door. We stood in a small white-washed room which was richly carpeted in Persian rugs. A small low couch lay to one side and on the pristine white wall hung a framed portrait of Freya Stark's muleteer in his wedding suit! Here, we were told, was the room where our explorer compatriot had stayed during her visit.

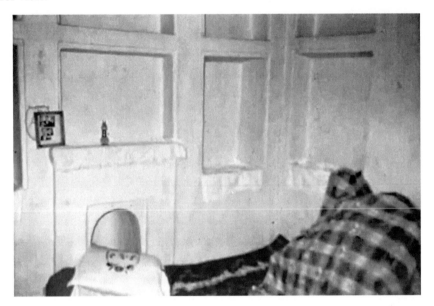

Freya Stark's Room at Garmarud

We returned to our rest place under the trees and made preparations for another night sleeping rough at this, our Camp 3 site. The flies were troublesome but we thought we could survive their onslaught. Our last action was to call the advance party on the radio to see how they were progressing. Unfortunately, the surrounding hills blocked our transmission and we could neither receive them nor they hear us.

Vic Last describes what befell the advance party on their journey to the Rock of Alamut:

"We left Garmarud at 1.45pm aiming to get as near to the Rock as possible before camping that evening. We chose to travel all the way down on the right-hand bank of the river. This was a mistake as the path often disappeared into villages and traversed steep scree slopes up to 150 feet above the river, whilst the track on the left-hand bank

looked good going. We passed through Zavarak and other villages before arriving at Shutur Khan at 6.50pm after a really hard push.

A villager offered to guide us to the local fresh water supply and led us up the river bed shown on Freya Stark's sketch map towards the Rock of Alamut. The Rock itself was not easily discernible in the fading evening light. After locating the spring about twenty minutes up river from the village our guide led us further up the valley with the apparent intent of feeding and sleeping us.

After about another twenty minutes walking, and having been shown the path up to the Rock, we insisted an orchard we were passing through would be suitable for a night stop and began to prepare a light meal. Ten minutes later our guide re-appeared with the owner of the land who warned us of the danger from snakes. He insisted we accompanied him and so we followed him to his house. There we were invited in and fed royally on local food. It was a fascinating experience to meet the farmer's family and learn something of the local customs. Our typewritten sheet of Persian words came in most useful as we attempted to converse with our hosts. Afterwards our farmer friend led us up to the flat roof of his house where we bedded down for a rather humid night's sleep.

25 June 1974

We left the house at 5.20am and began the hard flog up to the village of Qazir Khan which lies just below the Rock. The track crosses to the left-hand bank of the valley below the village, and the approach to the Rock of Alamut is made by passing through the village to tracks that are visible from below and appear to circuit behind the left-hand side of the Rock.

We had learned from our host the previous evening that the locals refer to the Rock as Qale Hassan – the Castle of Hassan. There was little evidence of the remains of the castle from a distance. However, the Rock itself is impressive and, in the wraiths of mist and low cloud which hung over it as we approached, it took on a very sinister and forbidding appearance. Its face was a wall of rock up to 1000 feet which rose vertically from the river bed and completely dominated the valley below. The Rock also effectively commanded the approaches into the valley from the mountains to the south.

The final climb up the rock was achieved by following a tortuous and difficult path up the left-hand side of the rear of the Rock. The path ends spectacularly in the mouth of a 30 feet tunnel cut through the Rock. At the other end we gained a panoramic view of the whole of the Qazir Khan Valley down as far as the Alamut Rud.

The ruins on the summit of the Rock were somewhat of an anti-climax. To a layman's eye they were probably not worth the effort of the climb. There was no wall standing which was higher than 6 feet, and for the most part the remains of Hassan's Castle consisted of heaps of rubble. However, our disappointment was compensated by the fantastic all-round panoramic view. As the cloud lifted, Alam Kuh was once again clearly visible to the east. The aesthetic feelings and views associated with our presence on the top of the Rock were worth an incalculable sum. All my party were agreed that the climb had been really worthwhile despite the physical effort we had expended in the process.

We left the castle at 9.10am and journeyed quickly through Shutur Khan reaching Shahrak by noon. In the Alamut Valley we followed the same route as the main party from Garmarud."

Rock of Alamut

Back at Garmarud, the day had started at the unearthly hour of 4am. Our mid-day rendezvous with the bus at Shahrak meant that we had to complete the long trek down the Alamut Valley in under 7 hours. By 5am the mules were loaded for the last time and we set off at a fairly fast pace down the now fairly wide riverside mule track. The sky was grey and overcast for the first time since leaving the Caspian, and some low cloud swirled around the rocks above Garmarud and obscured the view of the high peaks beyond. However, the somewhat gloomy cloud cover lifted during the morning to be replaced by blue skies and bright sunlight.

The scenery of the valley differed vastly from the forested regions we had traversed during the walk-in phase. The Alamut was a distinct example of valley cultivation in a rather dry and parched area. The surrounding hills were a red-brown and dusty looking terrain typical of the steppe which stretches all the way from the Anatolian Plateau to Afghanistan. In contrast, the valley floor was lushly cultivated by means of intensive irrigation.

The system of irrigation was itself fascinating. Numerous channels have been constructed to divert the waters of the Alamut Rud. In one place, an aqueduct which carried an irrigation channel effectively over the mule track consisted of little more than a hollowed out tree trunk.

The river banks were lined with Lombardy poplars, wild cherry trees and walnut trees. Villagers tilled cultivated strips along the banks and were growing crops varying from maize to opium poppy. Further downstream, we were to come across extensive acres of rice growing in flooded paddy fields. The bright green of the rice plants contrasted vividly with the dusty hills beyond.

By keeping up a fast pace, we reached the village of Zavarak and other small settlements fairly soon. The valley had now broadened considerably and the hill slopes on each side were as much as a mile apart.

It was near Zavarak that we spied some well-dressed Iranians moving around with dumpy levels, theodolites and sighting boards. We learnt that a route for a road was being surveyed. At this news we felt a little disappointed that civilisation would soon be coming to the remote Alamut Valley. Although such changes would obviously improve the lot of the villagers, they would doubtless change the pattern of life and, for example, the livelihood of the muleteers would be lost. In many ways we were glad to have visited the Alamut before it was overtaken by modernisation.

Further on towards Shutur Khan, some of us stopped for a while to examine an interestingly constructed mosque; a small, low, whitewashed building with rough-hewn wooden poles supporting a veranda at the front. In the centre was a white dome surmounted by an outstretched replica of a hand, with fingers pointing skywards. Evidently, this was symbolic of a place of worship in this area.

We established contact with the Alamut Rock party at the 10am radio call and learnt that they were all safe and had been successful in their venture. Delighted with this news, the mood of the party became quite jubilant. Cherryl even got around to making a radio call interspersed with excerpts from the 'Spam' song!

We by-passed the village of Shutur Khan and stopped for a rest at a wayside chaikhana. For the first time for ten days, we sat on chairs. These were arranged around a long table under the shade of a large tree. The Sergeant Major disappeared up the tree and we soon learnt why when we were showered with fruit – in appearance rather like a gooseberry. The Iranians called the fruit 'toots' and we soon realised we were sitting under a Mulberry tree.

Civilization had evidently reached this far since there was even a notice outside the chaikhana advertising 'tea' in English! The tea and ice-cold water mine host supplied was so refreshing we could have comfortably stayed there all day. However, we were concerned that if we were not at Shahrak when the bus arrived, the driver would depart without us and we would be stranded without transport.

The Alamut Rock team had not arrived at Shutur Khan by 10.30am, so the main party moved off. After a short journey along the river valley, the flat-roofed houses of Shahrak came into sight on a hill on the other side of some paddy fields. Eager to reach our goal, we broke into a fast pace. Most of us were puffing and had broken into a sweat by the time we reached the top of the slope up to the village. We collapsed into a small tea house by the side of the first road we had seen for days. The time was 11.30am and we celebrated the end of the route with many cups of refreshing 'chai'. Thirty minutes later the mules were sighted taking a track along the opposite side of the river from our approach route. 'Donkey Dawson' mounted the hill in solemn style to the cheers of the watchers from the tea house. Soon afterwards, he was followed by Vic Last and his team from the Rock of Alamut and the complete expedition was re-united at Shahrak.

We paid off the muleteers and bade them farewell. There was no sign of the mini-bus and so, our mountaineering mission completed, we relaxed the rule of no local food and ordered some Iranian dishes. It was a marvellous meal of yellow rice, eggs, tomatoes, yoghurt and chapattis. We all laughed and joked at the experiences of the last few days and enjoyed the first chance to really relax. It was good news that we had at last completed the long march and that our feet would not be subjected to further punishment!

The bus arrived at 1.30pm with a screech of brakes and narrowly missed hitting the wall of the tea-house. It was 1½ hours late. The driver explained that he had left Tehran at 6am and had been searching for Shahrak ever since. We had to admit that the village was extremely remote and that we were very fortunate he had found it at all.

The kit was soon loaded on the roof-rack. It seemed very strange to sit on the comfortable seats inside the vehicle. Nevertheless, before long we were bumping our way along the narrow dirt road that winds its way for mile after mile of the dry steppe and mountain country en route to Qazvin. On many an occasion the vehicle came dangerously close to the edge of a precipice as we rounded hairpin after hairpin bend. Several times too, we were enveloped in clouds of dust from a passing vehicle. To make matters worse, the driver insisted on refreshing his thirst from a bottle of Iranian vodka. Fortunately, he could handle the vehicle competently and we survived the ride.

All the while we travelled, the vehicle radio blared out incessantly. To our Western ears the repetitive bars of Iranian music sounded very monotonous. In contrast, our illustrious Captain appeared enraptured. He declared the words to be those of a beautiful Iranian love song and singer the best in Iran!

Near Qazvin we stopped at a wayside café and drank our first beer since leaving Akrotiri. This celebration pint was retrieved from the bottom of a small pond, which the café owner used as an open-air fridge for his bottles. Never had beer tasted so good to the weary and dusty group who climbed down from the bus!

It was 8.30pm before we reached Karadj and most of the team were fairly hungry. A halt was called at a wayside eating house and several bearded individuals (the girls excluded!) sat down to eat their first chelo-kebab. An enormous plate of rice was placed before us with meat and tomatoes. Only

Ray could manage to stagger through it – the rest of us had grown accustomed to eating less on the mountain.

We dropped our three Iranian colleagues at their barracks in Tehran and bade them farewell. Captain Ali promised to see us on the following day but the other two were uncertain what orders would await them. I made a short speech thanking them for their tremendous co-operation.

It was 10.30pm by the time we reached Gol-e-Sahra. Fortunately our previous camp site was vacant so we re-occupied it and, as before, slept in the open. Most of the team, before turning-in, took the opportunity to have their first shower for twelve days even though it was ice cold! I had to report to the British Embassy the next morning so I decided to shave the stubble from my chin. A groaning noise emerged from the washroom as I struggled with cold water and a blunt razor! The rest of the lads elected to remain bearded all except Doc John who managed to achieve a very clean-shaven appearance.

That night the heat of the plains was rather unbearable after the coolness of nights in the mountains. The inevitable ragging took place and the doc's lilo somehow managed to subside during the night. The majority opinion was that the 'Diddy men' were to blame but John took a rather different view the next morning!

6.   Overland Via Turkey

26 June 1974

We awoke quite early. As the mini-bus driver had worked very long hours the day before, we were not hopeful of the bus arriving punctually. Some of the braver expeditioners occupied the time by taking a plunge in the cold waters of Gol-e-Sahra Pool. The bus arrived at about 9am, much to the surprise of our two girls who were still splashing about in the water. Their sprint 'dripping wet' to the changing rooms produced a cheer from the lads! By now we had the technique of the loading of the roof rack down to a fine art and we swiftly formed a chain gang to move our kit on board.

Soon we were speeding through the city on the way to our first stop; the railway station. The Iranian State Railways had insisted we collect the tickets and presented our passports no later than 11am on the day before our departure. Ray and I nearly met a stumbling block at the station when officials there steadfastly refused to part with the tickets unless we first produced a receipt which had been obtained for us by an officer attached to the British Embassy staff. We realised too late that we had left this vital document in the Embassy. After much argument we managed to get the Station ticket clerks to agree to us presenting the receipt the following morning.

Our next step was to visit the British Embassy where we all made a rapid change from mountaineering clothes into more suitable attire for the journey through Turkey. Vic Last organized a packing session and transferred all our heavy equipment into boxes ready for air freighting back to Akrotiri. Meanwhile Ray and I visited Warrant Officer Thurbon of the Defence Attaché's staff to tell him of our safe return. Arthur Gooch was away on duty, but we left a small presentation plaque for him as a 'thank you' for his tremendous co-operation in the planning stages of the expedition. I also debriefed HM Defence Attaché, Group Captain Primavesi, on the achievements of the expedition. He seemed pleased it had been a great success. He promised to advise the British Ambassador and to officially thank the Iranian Army for their co-operation.

With tents and cooking stoves now left behind, we elected to stay in a reasonably cheap hotel at our own expense for the remainder of the time in

Tehran. The 'Passargad' was just such a hotel. It had been recommended to us by Captain Ali and was conveniently near his apartment in Tehran. After checking-in, it was time for shopping and sightseeing in the 'big city'. Locky was now suffering from similar problems to Roger and was confined to his bed. Peter Fields managed to get as far as the Bazaar before the 'tummy bug' caught up with him. Fortunately Doc John had a supply of suitable tablets which he readily dispensed.

At 7.30pm Captain Ali appeared and took Edi and Cherryl to his home to meet his wife and son. After a short while they returned and, clad in our 'best' travelling clothes, the team set out for a celebration chelo-kebab. Regrettably, Peter was still feeling groggy so we left him to get an early night.

Our meal was at the Hatam Juje Kebab House near the Vanak Hotel. At this pleasant open-air restaurant fountains played in ornamental pools which reflected the soft light from coloured lanterns suspended above. Captain Ali brought his wife and young son to the restaurant. It was also a farewell for them as the Captain had just been notified he was posted to an unaccompanied tour with the Iranian UN contingent in South Vietnam.

We were later joined by Mr Adili, Secretary, and Mr Rostani, Chief Climbing Instructor, of the Iranian Mountaineering Federation. They were both most interested in our exploits and Mr Rostani took copious notes on our climbing routes for a Press Release to local Tehran newspapers.

The highlight of the evening was reached when we presented Captain Aliary with a RAF Near East Air Force plaque as a token of esteem from the team for the tremendous assistance that he and his two companions had rendered to us. In a small speech, I said how sorry we were that Sergeant Major Zamanpour and Sergeant Regaie had been unable to join the celebration. I also stressed that without the efforts of Captain Aliary and his team, we could not possibly have achieved the same degree of success in our venture. After the formalities, the celebration continued until tiredness overcame the will to sample any more Iranian beer and wine.

27 June 1974

We were all up early and on our way to Tehran Railway Station well before 8am. Captain Ali appeared in his best uniform and insisted on presenting us with two enormous boxes of pistachio nuts for the journey. We were also delighted to see Sergeant Regaie who had managed to get time off to bid us farewell. Before boarding the train, we paused for a group photograph. Poor Roger was nearly arrested attempting this – unbeknown to us, railway stations are regarded as military installations in Iran and photography is strictly forbidden.

Tehran Departure

We waved our farewells from the Van Gulu Express as it pulled slowly out of Tehran Station at 9am. The promptness of the departure seemed to be a hangover from the days of the present Shah's father. His Imperial Majesty had established a reputation by personally checking that all public transport ran precisely on time. It was a pity that such good time keeping did not extend to trains across the Turkish border – as I had found out earlier.

The team settled down to look at the views from the compartment window in between bouts of eating and fitful dozing. We were fortunate to have secured two 6-seat first-class apartments to ourselves. The hard seats were not particularly comfortable, but they did have the advantage of sliding down to join the opposite seat so that a temporary bed could be made overnight.

Our travelling companions on the train were mainly Iranians but a few Turks, Americans, Austrians and Pakistanis mingled with them. The

Pakistanis were the most colourful and seemed to spend the whole of the journey clad in their white pyjama type trousers.

All day long the train followed poplar-lined river valleys through the yellow-brown steppe country. Many mud-walled houses were passed and occasionally we caught a glimpse of brightly dressed village women wearing styles typical of the region. The mountains in the background were often quite dramatic and as we approached Rezaieh, the area became very rugged with barren mountain peaks rising skywards in jagged confusion.

By now, night was falling fast and it was a strain to gaze at the scenery any longer. We turned our attention to the business of an evening meal and sleeping. The meal consisted of 'chicken and chips' – the sole choice on the dining car menu. Finding somewhere to sleep was fairly straightforward since at that stage there were several spare compartments and we could spread ourselves out.

Our peace was shattered when the train entered Tabriz at around midnight. A rising babble of voices from the platform outside warned us that we were just about to be invaded by many new passengers. We quickly withdrew to our reserved seats just in time. Even this was not enough for the noisy and angry crowd that boarded the train. Our compartment doors were rudely thrust open and we were accused of having taken other passengers' seats. Examination of our tickets showed this not to be so. However, it did not stop us from being sworn at in Persian, German, English and any other language that came to hand!

Our encounter with our fellow passengers also had its amusing moments. Eddy neatly deflated one individual in the middle of his ranting and raving by asking for a light. He was so taken aback by Eddy's audacity that he promptly stopped and offered him his lighter! On another occasion I announced to one particularly nasty customer that: "his manner was extremely rude and uncouth and that he should jolly well get lost!" We reinforced this message by using Eddy's boot to physically restrain any attempts to slide open the compartment door. After this we had no further trouble from the other passengers.

Just as we were drifting off to sleep, there began a succession of ticket and passport checks. Fortunately, no one had lost the magic pink forms and we were allowed to leave Iran without argument. On the Turkish side of the border the Customs officials' sole interest appeared to be in whether we were importing any electronic goods. They duly noted the number of our cassette recorder in Ray's passport and departed without further ado.

28 June 1974

When we began to stir, we discovered that the train was standing in a siding at the border station of Kapiköy. A few drab official buildings were grouped beside the track. The red crescent flag of Turkey fluttered from a solitary gendarmerie post. There was no sign of the train staff. Presumably they had gone off for prayers or breakfast in one of the station buildings. The problem was that the restaurant car had been taken off during the night and the passengers were left without any source of food and drink! We had wisely taken the precaution of packing a few tins of compo sweets and fruit in our rucksacks, so we managed a light breakfast.

Two hours later, the train moved slowly out of Kapiköy and began the journey to Van. It rattled along a single track which wound its way through mountain valleys to the edge of Lake Van. The villages we passed were equally colourful to those in Iran but there were now new sights to be seen. Bullock drawn carts with large solid wooden wheels trundled along dusty tracks. The village women wore brightly coloured voluminous dresses in contrast to the smocks and black trousers of Northern Iran. We were passing through an area inhabited by Kurdish tribes. The black tents of these nomads could occasionally be seen clustered on summer pastures or 'yaylas' as they are known in Turkey.

We arrived at Van some 2½ hours later. The water of the lake was calm and crystal-clear. As the coaches were shunted onto the train ferry, most of us gazed at the interesting silhouette of Van Castle with its medieval battlements strung out along the top of a nearby rock outcrop.

The journey across the lake was an experience. We spent some time on the boat deck gazing out across the waters of this vast lake towards distant snow-capped mountains on the far shore. The temperature was cool and refreshing which was perhaps not surprising for a lake at 5400 feet above sea-level. On the lower decks there was quite a contrast. In the first class saloon, an Iranian musician strummed out the music of his country on an instrument similar to a guitar. In the second-class saloon some Turkish national servicemen, clad in rough khaki serge uniforms, sang and danced to a Turkish melody. Young Iranian women in chadur and old Turkish ladies in full national dress with white veils mixed freely in the crowd. It was indeed a cosmopolitan scene.

The ship berthed at Tatvan on the far side of the lake after a voyage of nearly 4 hours. At Tatvan we were faced with a problem. For some inexplicable reason, it had only been possible to purchase tickets in Tehran for a journey as far as Van. From our previous experiences, we knew that there would be no peace that night if we did not retain our first-class compartments.

We had already purchased separate tickets for the lake crossing and, at Tatvan Station, Ray rushed out to buy tickets to Malatya. There we encountered our second problem – he could only obtain second-class tickets. Firm believers that 'possession is nine-tenths of the law' we re-occupied our first-class compartments and sat tight determined to argue our rights. Fortunately we were not disturbed and it was some twelve hours later before we had to pay the first-class excess on our tickets.

It was at Tatvan Station that we nearly lost two of the team. There was still no restaurant car attached to the train and we were feeling quite hungry by this time. Because of the uncertainty surrounding the train's departure, no one felt it wise to visit the Station café – some 30 yards away. However, as the train still showed no signs of movement an hour later, the Doc and Edi ventured out. A few minutes later the train started to move and we were just about to pull the communication cord when our missing pair jumped on the carriage steps – out of breath, but laden with cold drinks.

As it turned out, the train stopped a few hundred yards further on and spent the next two hours backing into the Station! As time drifted by, everyone became more and more ravenous. Eventually, Vic ventured out and, much to our joy, returned a short while later with a large amount of very greasy rice, some tomatoes and cucumbers and a few loaves of bread. There is nothing quite like hunger to create a good appetite, and it was not surprising that we ate our first Turkish meal with such relish. The bread was good and wholesome – a marvellous change from the rather doughy wafer-thin chupattis we had survived on in Iran. Meanwhile the train had still not re-started. We were all sound asleep by the time it eventually moved off.

29 June 1974

A restaurant car had re-appeared during the night – this time managed by Turkish staff. Some of us ventured down for a Turkish breakfast of bread, jam and çay (tea). The others brewed up their own mock-turtle soup which they ate with bread. The view outside had now changed to the gentler valley scenery of the central Anatolian Plateau. The towns we passed were distinctively Turkish; the domes and minarets of their mosques like smaller scale versions of Istanbul's famous Suleymaniye Mosque. Near Elazig, some excitement was caused when the train crossed over a large river. We were most interested to learn that this was none other than the great Euphrates of Biblical fame. Shortly after this, we ground to a halt in Malatya Station. The time was now 2pm and we were half a day behind schedule!

We moved our kit onto the platform and took the opportunity to buy fruit, bread and soft drinks from one of the many stalls on the platform. Ray and I made a rapid dash by dolmus (taxi-bus) to Malatya Bus Station but found that the only connection to Adana was just departing. A slower alternative was a 'postal' train departing for Yeniçe near Mersin at 3pm; so we settled for first-class tickets on this.

We sipped tea until our 'postal' pulled into the station. 'Steamed in' is a more appropriate description as the coaches were pulled by a powerful German built 2-8-2 locomotive of 1936 vintage. Black smoke and steam belched from this monster of the railroad and, for those old enough to remember, it was reminiscent of the days of steam in England.

The 'posta' as it is called in Turkish, pulled out of Malatya with much chugging, puffing and spinning of driving wheels. It was very different from the diesel-hauled Van Gulu express which had brought us from Tehran. The corridors were full of vendors selling anything from fruit and çimits (doughnut-shaped bread) to matches and penknives. The travelling sales boys seemed to journey from station to station, coming and going just as they pleased. In a way it was just like a travelling souk!

Often the train would stop for long periods at a solitary hut or building beside the track which was scarcely worthy of the name 'station'. Out of nowhere would appear a multitude of people – the men typically Turkish with their baggy trousers, flat caps and bristling mustachios; the women in coloured trousers and smocks with shoes that curled up at the toes. It was an education to study the scene as local peasants and farmers boarded the train with their goods – chickens in wicker baskets and vegetables of all descriptions.

Before long the rolling hills of the Anatolian Steppe gave way to the ruggedness of Turkey's Taurus Mountains. The light was fading fast as the sun sunk over the horizon; its rays bringing a soft orange glow to the narrow mountain valleys.

Our steam 'posta'.

The train frequently plunged into long tunnels and we found, to our cost, that travelling by steam train was a nostalgic event but one that had its own perils. The windows of our compartments were jammed in the down position and in every tunnel we were engulfed in black sulphurous fumes. After much coughing and spluttering, we would emerge from the far end of the tunnel with grit in our eyes, coal black faces and soot stained clothes!

It was almost completely dark when we came to a grinding halt at a remote settlement. With no forward motion of the train to cool us, we soon began to feel uncomfortably hot in the humid night air of Southern Turkey. Undaunted, Vic's compartment began a sing-song and soon they were joined by most of the remaining members. The noise of our singing attracted much attention from the local peasants, and before long the compartment was surrounded by a large crowd. All the team were extremely amused at their fascination – many Turks just stood before the compartment door and stared open-mouthed. One enterprising individual even climbed up the outside of the train to poke his head in the window; whilst another insisted on taping our choruses on a small cheap portable recorder.

30 June 1974

We had spent a hot and restless night as the train clattered along the track stopping at every tiny halt. As dawn broke, we were back once more in Mediterranean-type cultivation with its olives, carobs and citrus trees. The ramparts of an ancient castle on a distant rocky peak appeared to stand guard over the coastal plain between Ceyhan and Adana.

Our breakfast consisted of fresh fruit. Not long after eating this, our 'posta' reached Adana. It was then only a short journey to Yenice, a junction near Tarsus. At Yenice we again went through the process of unloading our kit by human chain onto the platform. It was at this stage that we realised our misfortunes. Eddy had woken up to find that money had been stolen from his wallet, and we now realised that our portable tape recorder containing an irreplaceable expedition tape had also disappeared. Evidently our so-called friends of the previous night had been somewhat light fingered! Fortunately we still had in our possession the principal tape cassette of the Freya Stark interviews.

Knowing it to be a hopeless situation, we nevertheless reported the theft to the Station Master. Our next problem arose when we attempted to board the connecting train to Mersin. This was a yellow and red painted 2-coach diesel rail car. As it entered Yenice Station we saw that it was already crammed to capacity and that some passengers were even hanging onto the carriage steps. It was evident that we stood no chance whatsoever of getting aboard. By this stage we were becoming rather bored with train travel but our sense of humour returned when a melon was commandeered for a quick game of rugby!

We had travelled too long and too far to be deterred by our failure to get on the train. Instead we investigated the road that ran past the station and managed to hail an ancient and ramshackle bus. By some stroke of genius, we crammed our kit aboard and travelled through Tarsus, the birthplace of Saint Paul, to Mersin.

On arrival at Mersin we were determined to try all modes of transport so we hailed a two-wheeled horse drawn cab known as a 'Peyton' in Turkey. Locky and the baggage were installed inside and cabman instructed to make full speed to the 'Ötel Bonjour' – a reasonable pension well known to Ray from his visit the previous year. We followed the clip-clopping of hooves and the jangling of horse brasses along the narrow streets to the Bonjour.

All modes of transport

Mine host welcomed the team and showed them to their shared rooms. There was a mad rush for the showers followed by attempts to remove the grime of train travel. The remainder of the afternoon was a chance to sightsee and shop. That evening we ate a superb fish meze at a seafront restaurant and washed this down with an excellent selection of Turkish red and white wines. Back at the hotel, the pleasant glow of the wine put us all in the mood to listen to the Doc's rendering of his humorous ditty on the expedition, and to read a more serious contribution by Vic Last; his ode 'King Solomon's Throne.'

1 July 1974

The next morning the hotelier at the Bonjour was most helpful and in-sisted on taking Ray and I to the office of Turkish Maritime Lines to confirm ticket reservations on the Mersin – Famagusta ferry. He also tried to locate the appropriate police department to report the theft of our cassette tape recorder. After trying several different police stations, we returned having been thwarted by bureaucracy and forced to abandon the attempt.

That afternoon, five of the team paid a visit to a local beach for a swim. They returned to the hotel at 6.45pm in time to load an ancient Chevrolet taxi which had been hired to take our kit to the ferry. The team walked the half mile to the harbour and queued to pass through the Customs and passport control desks. Regrettably, we were charged duty on the stolen cassette recorder – just to add 'salt to our wounds.'

We boarded the SS Truwa and had enormous difficulty locating our 4-berth cabins whose numbers appeared non-existent. In the search, Ray amused everyone by disappearing down one companionway at speed and becoming so disoriented that he re-appeared from the opposite direction having completed a full circle without even realizing it. Eventually, after negotiations with the Purser, we were all settled in our rightful abode.

It was a warm night and most of the party went up on deck and mingled with the crowds of Turkish Cypriots on board. Poor Eddy was suffering from a recurrence of the 'bug' and retired early to his cabin. For the rest it was time for a drink and to gaze out over Mersin's waterfront. The harbour was unusually full of navy ships – frigates, logistic support vessels and landing craft. At the time, we did not attach any undue importance to this. In the light of subsequent events in Cyprus, the presence of the Turkish Fleet was not so innocent as we had supposed!

We sailed at 8.30pm; for once on time. Most of us stayed on deck and watched the twinkling lights of Mersin disappear into the gathering gloom and the creamy wake of the ship which appeared phosphorescent in the moon-light. It was time to reflect on the events of the expedition – its successes and its near disasters. Time also to remember the friendships we had all made. We hoped they would be as long-lasting as the memory of the expedition itself.

2 July 1974

The voyage passed all too quickly and before we had been awake long the hotels of Famagusta were white pillars on the skyline. After berthing and a rugby scrum to get through Immigration Control, we again walked on Cyprus soil.

Although we were pleased to see the familiar white-painted RAF coach which was to convey us to Akrotiri, we could not help but feel a tinge of sadness that our great adventure had come to an end. We had achieved our objectives but we now had a lingering memory of the expedition and the challenges it had posed. The experience had changed all our lives and we would never forget it. Vic Last summarised our feelings in his poem: "King Solomon's Throne."

Epilogue

15 July 1974

Thirteen days later at dawn my wife and I woke up at RAF Akrotiri to the sound of intensive small arms fire. We rushed to the balcony of our married quarter and could see smoke rising from the Phassouri Plantation of orange groves just beyond the base perimeter. There was a strong smell of cordite in the air.

We subsequently learned that there had been a coup on the island of Cyprus. The President, Archbishop Makarios, had been overthrown by the Cypriot National Guard and EOKA B. What we were witnessing was fighting between them and supporters of Makarios.

The coup leaders were helped by the junta of generals ruling Greece and wanted union of Cyprus with Greece (Enosis).

20 July 1974

Turkey was concerned for the safety of the Turkish Cypriots in Cyprus and launched a full scale invasion on the north Cyprus coast at Kyrenia. The Cyprus war had started!

How lucky we were to have completed our expedition in time! Such a journey as we had just made from Tehran to Famagusta was now completely impossible.

King Solomon's Throne
a poem by Vic Last

Fireflies glow with eerie light,
Bullfrogs chorus paddy fields delight;
Curse the humidity of the night,
On to Alam Kuh.

Through rain forest lush and green,
Roaring torrent gives life serene;
Mules and men sweat as a team,
Working towards Alam Kuh.

Sleeping bodies 'neath a starfilledsky,
Dream of summits and ridges high;
Our guide, the river, still rushes by,
Down from Alam Kuh.

Final trek to Ab-e-Garm,
Base Camp one and springs so warm;
Snow-capped peaks stand proud and stern,
Guarding Alam Kuh.

Day of rest and recuperation;
Snake gives leader initiation;
To the trial and tribulation,
Protecting Alam Kuh.

Snowbridge over the joining rivers,
Marks the way to lofty wonders;
Haft Khan frowns on these intruders,
Challenging Alam Kuh.

Heart and lungs scream at the pressure,
Lack of oxygen who can measure;
Who the hell can call this leisure,
Fighting for Alam Kuh.

High camp now mid rock strewn splendour,
Sickness that altitude can render;
Sunset blows the mind with wonder,
Set for Alam Kuh.

Summit group departs alone,
Heavenward steps huge slabs of stone;
Haft Khan looks at Solomon's Throne,
Watching Alam Kuh.

Bodies aching, minds as one,
Ever upwards pushing on;
Break the ridgelines, all pain is gone,
God made Alam Kuh.

Standing still 'mid nature's glory,
Helpless to recount the story;
Of the meekness felt so strongly,
Seeing Alam Kuh.

Glacier feeding snowfilled valley,
Mount Korman calls, strength is rallied;
Rocky teeth along horsehoe alley,
Leading to Alam Kuh.

Nature's knife edged sword then flashes,
Alam Kuh's ridge its sharp teeth gnashes;
All hopes of progress there it dashes,
Aloof stands Alam Kuh

The mountain wins, but in the beating,
The mind transcends for moments fleeting;
To our place and of His teaching,
Au revoir Alam Kuh.

Now we leave this place of grace,
Nomadic peasant flocks take our place;
Such peace no chooser of creed or race,
Farewell to Ab-e-Garm.

Retracing steps, no time to ponder,
Backward glances, in awe and wonder;
Take in the tranquillity, the lightning, the thunder,
That makes up Alam Kuh.

Our guide the rushing snowmelt behind us,
Backbreaking climb out to ridgewalk stupendous;
Gay children, alternately bold and then nervous,
'Neath Maran's shady walnut bower.

Climbing now through spectacular gorges,
Rainbows through waterfalls cascading arches;
Glistening ribbon linking valleys with passes,
All the way down from Salambar.

Inert bodies lie 'neath a star filled sky,
Some full of sleep, some minds wondering why;
Satellites must track, shooting stars may fly,
Below the pass of Salambar.

Sandwich board blankets hide wiry muleteers,
The high pass beckons as dawn kills night's fears;
'Mid such beauty I contemplated my life's arrears,
My debts to God and man.

Scree strewn paths, feet are burning,
Stream twinkles below, throats are yearning;
Great boulders shade, cool rest earning,
As life goes babbling by.

Steepsided gorges closing in,
Eerie feelings of primeval sin;
Garmarud's ruined castle says 'no way in',
To the Valley of the Assassin.

Zavarak, Khushkedar, Shutur Khan,
Advance party nearing Qal-e-Hassan;
Bodies racked with fatigue, minds still strong,
Behold the Rock of Alamut.

Peasant family from out of the night,
Recognising weary travellers' plight;
Give food and comfort, warmth and light,
In their home in the Alamut Valley.

Wraiths of mist hiding phantoms dim,
Flat roofed village cowed by the sin;
Wrought in the name of Hassan the Assassin,
In the shadow of the Rock of Alamut.

Ruined castle on dizzy height,
Ravaged by the Mongol blight;
Centuries of watching peasants' plight,
Down the Alamut Valley.

Mist slithers away, sun welcomes our presence,
Ours is the rock, overcomes minds' resistence;
Rock tunnel's end frames cosmic experience,
Of the beauty that is Alamut.

Shahrak is calling – journey's end,
Through the veil of fatigue, feelings come, new friends;
Wills that have blended, waves that have passed,
Empty hands filled, sympathy given unasked.

At times minds diverse, blended as one;
Differing colours and codes having worked as one;
Indestructible feelings of a grace that binds,
But no words can echo the peace of mind,
Ringing out from those beautiful mountains.

Vic Last 1974

Appendix

Letters to Dr John Dove

The Expedition doctor, John Dove, wrote a short paper for the RGS to advise the Society of the achievements of the Solomon's Throne Expedition.

John also corresponded with Dame Freya Stark and copies of her original replies are reproduced at pages 98 to 101. It is interesting to note that she may have been the first person to have taken quinine into the Valley of the Assassins. Freya Stark wrote these letters at the age of 81.

John sent a rock he collected at Ab-e-Garm to the Department of Mineralogy at the British Museum (Natural History) and they analysed it. The findings are reproduced in the letter on page 102.

John also investigated the snakes in the Solomon's Throne area. A reply from the Institut d'Etat des Serums et Vaccins Razi in Teheran is reproduced on page 103.

c/o John Murray
50 Albemarle St. W1

11.9.74

Dear Dr Dove,

Your letter gave me much pleasure and would have been acknowledged long ago except that I was just going in for a hip replacement operation, now happily over - I am now hoping that this may reach you in view of what is happening in Cyprus, and would be glad to have a word of its safe arrival. Very glad too to think that you are going to explore the lovely valley & those mountains. before the motor roads come to spoil them - It gives

Letter from Freya Stark dated 11 September 1974 (page 1)

me a strange feeling to think that
so many years have passed & have
brought so little change.

My letters are being published,
a volume at a time, and the Vol. II
(on the Persian journeys) should
come out next spring in time for
you to take, for I do not suppose
you would be going before May? I will
send you a copy if you let me know
the address or that this reaches you

Yours with every good wish

Freya Stark

Letter from Freya Stark dated 11 September 1974 (page 2)

Dear Dr Dove,

Thankyou so much for sending your RGS paper;I
have been reading it with great pleasure,and feeling
young again with those lovely valleys opening out before
my memory. I am glad to think that you are going again,
and hope you will be able to give a careful look to both
castles that held the two valley entrances: I missed the
one above Badasht (being very ill when I heard of it)
but Nevisar was well worth a visit and held the valley
I feel sure, although an expedition a few years ago
(who did not get up to it) proposed another castle whose
name I have forgotten. Mr Ivanoff who is the authority
on the Ismaili, is however definite that Nevisar held
the Alamut ,and I think it is obvious . I think you
must go down the river to Lambesar, which is a fine
castle with walls still in good order (in 1931 !), and
as I lost all my photographs there I should love to look
at anything you collect.

I like your paper very much; it is pleasant reading
and gives all the information, and am of course very xix
pleased to find a sharer in my view of exploration.
Your reasons for going are of course excellent. Maps
troubles:every traveller in the M.East will sympathise
with. I expect the German altitudes are correct: I
had to struggle with a constant wind that made my little
"Abney Level" instrument very unmanageable.

I believe I first took quinine to the valley : no
one had heard more than vague rumours of it, and I am
glad to know that health is now looked after.

I can tell you what the 'tut' berries were:white
mulberries, and very refreshing! The galoches are xxxx
rather sad to think of, but perhaps you may still find

Letter from Freya Stark dated 3 January 1975 (page 1)

the cotton ' giva ' which is as good a footwear as you
can have for those paths and rocks.

I must not wander on like this, but only add all
good wishes for your next season. Do please let me know
how it goes.

I enclose the notice of my Letters;the Ist vol is
now out and covers 1930 ; 1931 and the second journey
should come out this year in ~~autumn~~ summer. It is better
for you to write direct as posts between Italy and England
are hopeless just now. I used to write to my mother
every day so that they do cover all the detail of the
journeys.

I enclose a little summary and hope it is what
you wanted; if not ,do not hesitate to tell me and I can
alter it, *or take anything out as you think*

With so many thanks for giving me the pleasure
of sharing your expedition,
   Yours sincerely,

Freya Stark

*I should love to see a narrative
of the trip -*

Letter from Freya Stark dated 3 January 1975 (page 2)

Telegrams: *Nathismus, Southkens, London*
Telephone: 01-589 6323

BRITISH MUSEUM (NATURAL HISTORY)
Cromwell Road
London, S. W. 7

DEPARTMENT OF MINERALOGY

AJC/NMG/856/6

5th August 1974

Dr John Dove,
PM Hospital,
R.A.F., AKROTIRI,
BFPO 53.

Dear Dr Dove,

I expect our Zoology Department will have written to you, or will write to you, concerning the snake you described in your letter of the 7th July.

The rock you sent us from Ave Garm is a quite typical product of a "hot" spring. It consists predominantly of calcite ($CaCO_3$), much stained and coated with (X-ray) amorphous iron oxide, with minor amounts of discrete crystallised goethite ($FeO(OH)$) occupying the interstices of the individual calcite grains. These grains are cemented by the iron oxides and by the mineral barytes $BaSO_4$. Your description of the sulphurous smell accords with the presence of the last named mineral:- sulphur (mineral) itself is usually to be expected only at higher temperatures than the water you describe.

It is probable that the water was rich in ionic sulphur/sulphate which may have been derived from the oxidation of a sulphide body through which the spring water passed. This would conveniently explain the high temperature of the water since such sulphides on oxidation release heat.

The other possibility is that this spring is primary, obtaining both heat and salts from some igneous mass at depth, or from some faulted resevoir of preexisting liquid.

I hope this is of some help to you, and it is quite in order for you to publish any of the information. Your specimen is returned herewith.

Yours sincerely,

A. J. Criddle.

***ENCLOSURE

Letter from British Museum, August 1974.

INSTITUT D'ETAT DES SERUMS ET VACCINS RAZI

Boîte postale 656 Téhéran

HESSARAK - KARADJ (IRAN) Adresse télégraphique. LABHESSARAK - TEHERAN

August 18, 1974

Dr. John Dove
PM Hospital
RAF Akrotiri
BFPO 53
England

Dear Dr. Dove;

       In response to your letter dated August 4, 1974;
I would like to inform you that as far as I know only two species
of venomous snakes (Vipera xanthina and Vipera lebetina) are
occurs in Solomon's Throne area of Albburz mountains in Iran.
The observed information of your letter showed that the snake
should be Vipera lebetina. The correct identification of the snake
only available by examination of the specimens.

Yours sincerely

Dr. M. Latifi
Head of Herpetology and Antivenins Dept.

Letter from Dr Latifi in Tehran, August 1974.

Acknowledgements

Thanks are due to the Royal Air Force for providing air transport and administrative support for the expedition.

Thanks are due to the Defence Staff of the British Embassy, Tehran, for their valuable assistance to the expedition.

Thanks are due to the 1st Battalion Special Forces of the Iranian Army for their professional help with the day-to-day operation of the expedition and for providing its security.

My thanks to Vic Last for giving permission to reproduce his poem 'King Solomon's Throne' at pages 93 to 96.

My thanks to John Dove for giving permission to reproduce the letters he received in the Appendix.

My thanks to Ray Condon and Mike Dawson for reading and correcting the original text.

Bibliography

Stark, Freya, *The Valleys of the Assassins*, John Murray, London 1934
Willey, Peter, *The Castles of the Assassins*, Harrap, 1963
Fiennes, Ranulph, *Atlantis of the Sands*, Bloomsbury, London 1992